The Witches' Key to the Legion

A Guide to Solomonic Sorcery

REVISED AND EXPANDED

The Witches' Key

The Witches' Key to the Legion

A Guide to Solomonic Sorcery

REVISED AND EXPANDED

L.M. Black

Asteria
Books

Editor: L.M. Black
Author: L.M. Black
Illustrators: J. Blackthorn, L.M. Black
Cover Art: J. Blackthorn

The Witches' Key to the Legion: A Guide to Solomonic Sorcery
Revised and Expanded Edition

ISBN: 9781956765007 (paperback)

Keywords
1. Goetia 2. Legion 3. Solomonic Magic 4. Witchcraft 5. Sorcery 6. Demonology

Copyright © 2013, 2021 by Asteria Books

Notice of Rights: In accordance with the U.S. Copyright Act of 1976, the scanning, uploading, and electronic sharing of any part of this book without the permission of the publisher is unlawful piracy and theft of the author intellectual property. If you would like to use material from this book (other than for review purposes), prior written permission must be obtained by contacting the publisher at laurelei@asteriabooks.com. Thank you for your support of the author's rights.

Notice of Liability: The author has made every effort to check and ensure the accuracy of the information presented in this book. However, the information herein is sold without warranty, either expressed or implied. Neither the author, publisher, nor any dealer or distributor of this book will be held liable for any damages caused either directly or indirectly by the instructions and information contained in this book.

Permissions: For information on getting permission for reprints and excerpts, contact: submissions@asteriabooks.com

Disclaimer: Information in this book is NOT intended as medical advice, or for use as diagnosis or treatment of a health problem, or as a substitute for consulting a licensed medical or mental health professional. The contents and information in this book are for informational use only and are not intended to be a substitute for professional medical advice, diagnosis, or treatment. Always seek the advice of your physician or other qualified health provider for medical conditions. Never disregard professional medical advice or delay in seeking it because of something you read in this book or any spiritual resource.

For S
and my Friends on the Other Side

"Come, high or low;
Thyself and office deftly show!"

The Wyrd Sisters, William Shakespeare

Contents

Foreword by Bill Duvendack	i
Preface to the Revised and Expanded Work	v
Introduction	vii

Commentaries

On Creating a Key for Witches	3
On Unlocking the Key	7
On Goetic Magic and Evocation	11
On Models of Magic	15
On Evocation, Invocation, and Banishing	19
On Spheres and Pyramids	23
On Affinity Between Witch and Spirit	25
On Care and Keeping of Familiars	27
On the All and the Adversary	29
On the Creation of the Legion	33
On the Meaning and Use of the Seals	37
On Solomon's Ring & Legacy	41
On the Greater Legion	43
Demonic DO NOT CALL List	45

Goetic Correspondences	49
Areas of Influence and Interest	55

The Conjurer's Craft

Tools of Conjuration	69
Aligning the Three Souls	99
Cleansing, Shielding, and Banishing	105
Laying the Compass & Building the Pyramid	123
Invitation & Departure	129
Methods & Techniques of Spirit Communication	133
The Compact	155
The Vessel	159
Offerings	165
In Case of Emergency	171

The 72 Spirits

1. Bael	184
2. Agares	192
3. Vassago	198
4. Samigina	202
5. Marbas	206
6. Valefor	210

7. Amon	214
8. Barbatos	218
9. Paimon	224
10. Buer	232
11. Gusion	236
12. Sitri	240
13. Beleth	244
14. Leraje	250
15. Eligos	254
16. Zepar	258
17. Botis	262
18. Bathin	266
19. Sallos	270
20. Purson	274
21. Marax	280
22. Ipos	284
23. Aim	288
24. Naberius	292
25. Glasya-Labolas	296
26. Bune	300
27. Ronove	304
28. Berith	307

29. Astaroth	314
30. Forneus	322
31. Foras	326
32. Asmoday	330
33. Gaap	336
34. Furfur	342
35. Marchosias	346
36. Stolas	350
37. Phenex	354
38. Halphas	358
39. Malphas	362
40. Raum	366
41. Focalor	370
42. Vepar	374
43. Sabnock	378
44. Shax	382
45. Vine	386
46. Bifrons	390
47. Uvall	394
48. Haagenti	398
49. Crocell	402
50. Furcas	406

51. Balam	410
52. Alloces	414
53. Camio	418
54. Murmur	422
55. Orobas	426
56. Gremory	430
57. Ose	434
58. Amy	438
59. Oriax	442
60. Vapula	446
61. Zagan	450
62. Valak	456
63. Andras	460
64. Haures	464
65. Andrealphus	470
66. Kamaris	474
67. Admusias	478
68. Belial	482
69. Decarabia	488
70. Seere	492
71. Dantalion	496
72. Andromalius	500

Parting Resources

Acknowledgements — 505

Appendix A — List of Figures — 507

Appendix B — Resources — 511

Glossary — 515

Bibliography — 523

Index — 522

About L.M. Black — 531

About J. Blackthorn — 533

Also from Asteria Books — 535

Foreword

Witch. W.I.T.C.H. Do you know the definition of the word? According to the Oxford English Dictionary, it is "a woman thought to have magic powers, especially evil ones, popularly depicted as wearing a black cloak and pointed hat and flying on a broomstick." The Merriam-Webster Dictionary is fairer: "a person (especially a woman) who is credited with having usually malignant supernatural powers." Then it goes on in a latter point to define what most of us know: "a practitioner of witchcraft especially in adherence with a neo-pagan tradition or religion (such as Wicca)." At least they get it partially right! Both of these fall far short of the mark in describing a witch, though, because the word is undefinable in some ways.

That last point is why I took the time to share the definitions above. This book, *The Witches' Key to the Legion: A Guide to Solomonic Sorcery*, is a book that was needed to be written when it was released many years ago. Very few books released before it blended the two different worlds of the witch and the ceremonial magician, and the ones that did, did not go into this level of depth and detail regarding the Goetia that this tome did. Besides connecting spiritual paradigms, it also offered another perspective on centuries-old information, a concept after my own heart!

Here we are, ten years later, and like things that are true and real, evolution has happened. The book industry's evolution to start to include more books like this is the first evolution that comes to mind, but a second one is lurking in the shadows. The second point of evolution is simply the work done with the spirits and the material in this book *over the last ten years!* This research has led to many additions in the present volume, including artwork, expanded commentaries, and a broader collection of practical tools and techniques. The latter point makes it an autonomous work for goetic magick aimed at the witch. I particularly enjoy that.

There have been more and more of these "hybrid" books released in the last ten years. They're not hybrid in a strict sense of the word, but rather cross-pollinated, and the fact I have to take the time to explain that is testament to the necessity of this book and similar ones. The human mind has a usually subconscious tendency to label and organize things, which generally works in our favor, but sometimes does not. It works in our favor when we learn what is poisonous and what is not, but it works against us here. Too many times, as Laurelei explains in her introductory remarks, books written about the Goetia have been aimed at ceremonial magicians, making them cumbersome to work with outside of that particular paradigm. As we develop through life, our mind does shift into a "this belongs here, and that belongs there" mindset, and this tenth-anniversary edition of *The Witches' Key to the Legion* reminds us to question that process every day of our lives. Why can't the Goetia be worked with by witches in their style? Is it going to hurt the feelings of some dead white guy somewhere in the old world? I can tell you from decades of personal experience that the spirits don't care if you're a witch, magician, Gandalf, or Houngan, and if you think they do, this book may not be for you…yet. But one day in the future, it will be, and when that day arrives, may you enjoy it as thoroughly as many before you.

The timely release of this edition so close to the Grand Conjunction reminds us that it is a new century, and as we look at the world around us, we can safely and confidently say that the majority of the old ways no longer work. Evolution and fine-tuning our mental labeling faculties are wise to make a lifelong learning process as we navigate these transitionary times. Thank the Gods Laurelei has put this book together so that we don't have to do the work here, too! This book fills a niche, and its tenth anniversary stands as a testament to the quality of what is contained herein.

Whether you are a witch that wants to learn about and work with the Goetia or a ceremonial magician that is always open-minded enough to look at established ideas from an innovative and evolved perspective, there is something of value here for you. Well, I guess there is. I mean, there was for me and all of the readers who made this tenth-anniversary edition possible.

So, sit a spell. Grab your drink in your favorite reading chair, and curl up with this good book for an afternoon. Enjoy the added material that makes it more self-contained, and be sure to take notes on what you see and what has been added. Then, most importantly, give thanks for Laurelei and this book, as it shows you the ghost-light path concurrent to our path, the crooked. This is a fantastic book that will continue to show its value for decades, if not centuries, to come because it was the first. It does not get more innovative than that.

Bill Duvendack

Walpurgisnacht 2021

Preface

This book is intended for Witches. It is unusual in that regard. Looking at the current range of books on the topic of Goetic Spirits and Goetic Magick, most are addressed to a very different sort of audience — one with a very different approach to magick, Spirits, and the world of the Unseen.

Witches, particularly Traditional Witches, tend to cultivate a practice that is informed by folklore, medieval grimoires, the practices of pre-modern sorcerers as attested in trial records and other historical accounts, teachings from mentors, and first-hand experience. That direct experience (what some might call UPG — Unverified Personal Gnosis) of Godds, Spirits, magick, and sorcery often makes for a very individualized experience, which is why it can be so easy for practitioners of paths that rely heavily on scholarship and citations to dismiss our work as crude and untested, and so easy for us to keep our great wisdom to ourselves, for ourselves. I get it. I am often nervous about sharing my work with the class, for fear that what has been meaningful to the point of profundity for me will be disregarded (or worse — mocked) by the folks who are so lauded for their conventional thought on the topics.

And then the Spirits speak, and they remind me that every Mage and Witch whose work is now the foundation of some branch of esoterica was once a Mage or Witch alone, recording their work for their own benefit or daring to share this new thought that others might find some Light of Truth to help inform their practice. I offer, then, my own thoughts, my own practice, my own work in the same spirit, that other Witches will either find confirmation for practices and beliefs they have felt isolated in their practice of, or that they will be inspired to try a new practice or test an old belief in light of a spark offered here.

The idea for this book was born in 2011 and 2012, as my now-ex-wife and I entered the beginnings of our workings with certain Spirits among the Legion (the 72 Spirits of the Goetia). I will discuss more of our process in those years, and my process in the intervening years, in the commentary entitled "Unlocking the Key." However, in speaking here about how the book came to be, I will say plainly that there were these motivations: a Spirit with whom I built great trust and affection asked me to write the book and suggested that I direct it to Witches; most of the Witches with whom I have discussed the Spirits of the Legion before, during, and since that time feel an apprehension that I believe is ingrained by Abrahamic doctrine and which is in desperate need of undoing; and, finally, I recognized that my own knowledge was somewhat limited on the topic of the Goetia, but I didn't find any resources on the market for a practitioner like myself. A Witch.

The original printing didn't quite hit its mark, though. While it conveyed in the strongest possible terms the need to eschew the "Spirit torture" that was a hallmark of other manuals on demonology, and was therefore considerably more in alignment with Witchcraft sensibilities, it assumed a level of knowledge and practice of Spirit-work techniques on the part of the reader that may or may not have been present — and left the poor Witch without any tools or techniques if they hadn't brought those with them. It whet the appetite, but it left one hungry.

This current edition, undertaken a decade after the original work was begun, has been revised and hugely expanded so the reader can feast!

Introduction

γοητεία goēteia – charm, jugglery
γόης goēs – charmer, enchanter, sorcerer
δαίμων daemon – nature spirit
δαίω daio – to divide (destinies)

It is almost impossible (and would certainly be incomplete) to approach a discussion of Goetic Magick without also mentioning Theurgy— and how the two have been intermixed in the mind and work of prominent magickal practitioners and authors since Aleister Crowley and his work. It is not entirely my purpose to educate the reader on what Theurgy is, nor do I want to frame Goetia simply in terms of what it is not. However, since some readers will come to this current work with vast knowledge of other Goetic texts (and will naturally be drawn to compare this with those) and other readers will have no prior knowledge (but will be inspired to continue their studies with other authors), it seems prudent to set the stage just a little.

In its shortest possible definition, Theurgy is a branch of magickal practice in which the practitioner utilizes rituals and formulas in order to align with Divine Powers — the Godds. It is generally viewed as a mystical experience, and many contemporary Mages write about it as the supreme (or "highest") expression of magick.

Thaumaturgy is a branch of magic that is concerned with the "working of miracles" — or achieving practical results, often through communication with "higher order" beings (Godds, Angels, etc).

Goetia, by contrast, is sorcery, plain and simple. It is considered "low" magick because practitioners who utilize it call upon "lower order" beings (daemons … demons … Spirits) to achieve mundane or practical ends.

All of this talk of "high" and "low" in terms of magickal goals and types of beings can be traced back to Platonism, Hermeticism, and Neoplatonism (and maybe even further back to Zoroastrian dualism, depending on who you ask). It doesn't serve us, for this work, to get mired in a discussion of these philosophies, but it is important to understand the barest of their bones in order to frame our discussion.

According to Hermetic and Neoplatonic thought, all of reality emanates from a singular source. The First, the Highest, the One, the Monad. If you consider this primary source as the purest good and the highest high, the whitest white, and the bestest best, then everything that projects (emanates, extends, derives) from it is just a little less good, less high, less white, less best. Each layer of emanation gives way to the next, and each next is a little less of what the One is. Ultimately, all of the superlatives of the time are attributed to the One at the top end of the spectrum, and all of their opposites are at the other end.

And all the opposites are necessarily bad. Evil. Malevolent. Low. Black. Inferior.

Celestial = good. Earthly = bad.

Spiritual = good. Physical = bad

High = good. Low = bad.

Light/White = good. Dark/Black = bad.

Masculine = good. Feminine = bad.

Goetia as a practice calls on Spirits that are a step above this earthly manifestation. They are higher on the ladder of emanations than we are, to be clear, according to this line of thought. They don't have to muck around with bodies and excrement and anything physical unless they choose to. This is better than human existence which is bound up in an earthly shell — again, according to this type of philosophy.

I'm going to be honest: I have issues with this philosophy. I know it is ancient, and I know it is the foundation of nearly all of what is termed "modern magick." So much of Witchcraft has come to rely on this dualism, and I am not sure that it serves us well as a People. In fact, I know it can't. Racism and sexism are baked in — along with a number of other troubling ideas that are too complex to undertake here.

We won't be doing Theurgy as part of this current work.

Please don't misunderstand, though. I have no issue with Theurgy or its goals. It is good and proper in its place and time, and both it and Thaumaturgy are utilized in Witchcraft. It is Neoplatonism and Hermeticism and other dualistic paradigms that I find problematic.

We won't be getting Theurgy in our Goetia because I have no desire to obscure the potency and availability of the Goetic Arts. I choose to present it to you as it is. Rich and potent and present like fertile soil.

We are Witches – weavers of "Grey Magic" which blends the (so-called) high and the low, light and dark within one vessel. We know them all to be potentially positive (the luscious and cool dark embrace of night) and potentially negative (the obliterating white-hot blast of a bomb). We embrace our physical natures and experience, and we do not deny the physical realm or the Underworld their proper places in preference of the "upper" (or celestial) world.

In many cultures where shamanism is practiced, spiritual movement takes place in three planes, worlds, or realms. The three realms are the World Above (the sky, heaven, land of the Godds, the celestial plane), the World Between (the land, middle-earth, place of the elemental gates, land of the nature Spirits, the physical plane), and the World Below (the sea, the underworld, land of the Dead, the demonic plane). It is within us, as Witches and weavers of the Wyrd, that the these worlds mix and marry.

Furthermore, I believe that Crowley and Mathers did no favors for the daemons in this book by popularizing their conjuration with the sort of abusive exorcisms and other rituals that they presented for public consumption. These Spirits are not all monsters bent on evil deeds. The ones who are, you would be wisest never to call, even with the supposed aid of elevated magickal structures. Torture and bondage, if you are indeed capable of binding these beings, have only wrought the effect of making many Spirits resentful of interacting with us.

My ex-wife and I initially undertook this work at the request of the Spirits with whom we consort, and I have continued in the years since our separation. My greatest guide and teacher in this current work is a member of the Legion. She has communicated a wealth of wisdom – both practical and theoretical – via talking boards, automatic writing, and scrying. She has been friend and mentor to me and the to the members of my Coven, shining a light into the world of shades so that we might bring you accurate and useful insights into Spirit work.

Nor has she been the only guide from within the Legion to inform this work. (More on that when we come to "Unlocking the Key.")

If you are familiar with prior editions of the Ars Goetia and other works of demonology that treat on these same Spirits, you will undoubtedly recognize some differences in the descriptions included in this "New Key." Here you see my guide's insight and knowledge and how it adds to the lore and practical partnerships offered by each Spirit.

What you will not find in this book are repetitive rituals that sling threats and abuse upon the Spirits. Many of the Spirits here require a "firm hand and a strong Will," but they will actively re-sent being insulted, threatened, and tortured, as has happened for the last several centuries. Indeed, Spirit torture has been the norm since the printing of the many medieval grimoires, and it is attributed to Solomon himself. I do not hold truck with this practice. I find it unethical and completely unnecessary. I hope to present here a reasonable and useful alternative for Witches and all others who hope to step away from such abuse.

Did Solomon actually form the Legion of 72 Spirits and write a book concerning their control? That is a doubtful historical scenario, and yet the lore among Mages long ago established it as a sort of "Energetic Truth." Whether it is literally true or not, Solomon's involvement with the Spirits of the Legion has been canonized to the point that even many of the Spirits believe (and claim to "remember") it as a fact. Because it is, at this point, "as good as true" from a spiritual/energetic perspective, we will be writing about Solomon in this capacity throughout this work.

Whether Solomon or other magicians who followed him by centuries were the initiators of Spirit torture, it is clear that the Spirits of the Legion have suffered too long at the hands of sadistic "masters." Some of these Spirits are now dangerous and shouldn't be called upon at all.

In this *Witches' Key to the Legion*, I have explored the Legion as it exists today. With the help of Familiar Spirits from within the ranks, I offer you descriptions of the Spirits and their sigils, practical advice for working with these beings, history and lore related to the creation of the Legion, and a complete Demonic DO NOT CALL List.

The short editorial commentaries that serve to complement this work ("On the All and the Adversary," etc.) are discussions that came out of the original (2011-2012) exploration of the 72 spirits of the Legion.

In this revised and hugely expanded edition, I have sought to include more comprehensive commentaries, a complete and thorough discussion of tools, techniques, formulas, and rituals for Goetic magick and communication, a cleaner format for the Spirit index, and back matter that will make the entire work easier to access (including a glossary, bibliography, appendices, and index).

The art has also been updated and refreshed. The work of J. Blackthorn still takes pride of place on the cover and throughout the work, but classic illustrations from medieval grimoires and my own photo collages add a visual lexicon for the reader's understanding of nearly every Spirit.

When I began this work (with my ex-wife and our Coven), the information was largely unknown to us. Some is unverifiable — and may remain so. Every morsel (and I have tried to make explicit which morsels are additions to the corpus of classical work) was given directly from guides within the Legion.

As always, you are at liberty to make your own judgments and test this information against your own practice. As Lon Milo Duquette said, from his own treatment on the Goetia: "One who has never experienced a Goetic Evocation is not qualified to voice even the most educated opinion on the subject. It is one thing to be well-read on a subject; it is quite another to be part of the subject itself. " Put this information into practice, and judge for yourself.

I hope that the information contained herein will be of value to you in your magical practice. More than that, I hope that you forge lasting relationships with one or more Spirit and that you accomplish together all your many goals.

Commentaries

On Creating a Key for Witches

I have a few reasons for targeting this book to Witches and not, say, Ceremonial Magicians. The first is that every other available book that treats on these 72 Spirits and the nature of their work is aimed at Ceremonial Magicians. Those books are edited by illustrious members of prominent magickal Orders, and they assume a certain familiarity with the working systems espoused by the same. The editorial essays and commentary are excellent in their scholarship; and they are, for the most part, solid reference resources for most practitioners — with a few being truly top shelf. I especially recommend Lon Milo DuQuette's *Illustrated Goetia*.

However, they continue to advocate Spirit torture as the de facto mode of operation. That torture generally follows this pattern: bind a Spirit into a physical object, command it to do the task you desire, threaten to harm the Spirit if they don't comply, progressively inflict greater harm on the Spirit through the use of magickal formulas and the exposure of the binding object to a flame. It is horrific. It is often based on a history of misogyny and xenophobia (since many of these Spirits were well-known Goddesses and land Spirits of other cultures). It is based on slaving culture and the inherent "right" of certain powerful men to own and control anyone they deem as "lesser." And it is a "given" standard of practice that most of the world's occultists don't question and certainly don't publicly contradict. Only a rare few are starting to come forward with alternatives.

Of all the resources and references on this group of 72 Spirits, none have been written for Witches (until the first edition of this book), which is ironic given the meaning of the words γοητεία (goēteia) and γόης (goēs). The Greek word "goēs" (pronounced like GO-ays) means "sorcerer" or "charmer" or "enchanter" and is associated with the type of magick that Witches historically have always done. Namely, calling upon Spirits to assist with worldly workings with material-plane goals.

This "New Key" is for Witches specifically because it has been the role of the Witch to summon and stir Spirits as allies since Witches first started practicing their Craft. This IS sorcery. We see evidence of the deep connection between Witches and Spirits in folklore, trial records, art, and (when we feel brave enough to share our Spirit-based experiences) among others within the contemporary Witchcraft community.

Sadly, contemporary Witches have been made to feel cut-off from Spirit-work — and have been made to fear Spirits with whom we have previously found affinity, friendship, passion, and partnership. The word "demon" itself is often enough to turn away a Witch's interest, having been fed (and swallowed) the Abrahamic lie that demons are evil, by virtue of being a demon.

The work of the *Ars Goetia* (and related works like the *Pseudomonarchia Daemonium* and other grimoires that catalog Spirits) have been taboo for many Witches since Wicca and Witchcraft came out of the shadows and into public view in the 1950's when Britain's anti-witchcraft laws were repealed. Only the Godds of the Witches were discussed, and even then, only in terms and forms that wouldn't frighten the public too badly. The White Goddess. The Horned God. (Not the Queen of Heaven and Hell. Not the Devil. Although these are titles for the same two Powers.)

I am a Witch, working independently and in a Coven. I am professional psychic reader, as are several of the people with whom I have shared Coven bonds. One common thread that we have seen in our own lives, in our Coven, and in the experience of our clients is that we humans are spiritual beings having a human experience. We are Spirits enfleshed, and we walk within a world of ethereal Spirits who act as guides, guardians, and aides to us, often whether we are aware of them or not. We have gotten on the talking board numerous times with family and friends to find a helpful Spirit has been by their sides since childhood or adolescence.

People find comfort in knowing that they are not alone, even if they cannot see their circle of friends because they dwell in Spirit. More than that, Witches find companions in magic among the Spirits familiar to them (Spirit Familiars).

This current work is a giant step forward for the practicing Witch in discovering the entities who inhabit the Unseen Realms and in uncovering the means to communicate and work with them.

On Unlocking the Key

A work such as this (one that is not a just a look at classical material from a new angle, but which also includes information that was gained directly from many of the Spirits who are the subjects of discussion) would be incomplete without providing some insight into how that work was done and over what scope of time.

My first conscious contact with any of the Spirits of the Goetia happened in 2011. I had begun talking board sessions (on my own, at this point) to reach out to Spirits who I felt were making attempts at communication, and the Spirit who came through the strongest identified themselves as "S."

My now-ex-wife and I engaged in a lot of talking board communication starting around that time. As I became acquainted with S, she took on the role of "Gatekeeper" for my partner and me. My partner's Spirits also made themselves more known, and they helped her with the energetic part of the work.

By early 2012, we had come to know S as one of the 72 Spirits of the Goetia — though S told us that "Legion" was a preferred term among the Spirits themselves. They didn't particularly care for the name "Goetia," which (among other interpretations) means "Howling." I knew which Spirit among the 72 that S was, although she let me know that she didn't like being called by the names listed for her in the book (due to abuse, mispronunciation, and her own personal taste), and she asked instead that I just call her "S" most of the time.

With S as our most vocal and omnipresent guide, my partner and I started asking questions about the Legion in general, and then about specific Spirits. By 2012, we were engaged in a series of systematic conversations about each Spirit, in order as presented, with the occasional "deep dive" into related topics and questions that occurred to us or were suggested by S. Those deep dives have become the foundation for the Commentaries in this book.

Our method was relatively simple. We laid our Compass, invited S to speak with us through the talking board, and recorded everything using either micro-cassettes or the voice recorder on my phone. We did not, at that time, utilize a Triangle of Art.

We did, however, get the benefit of talking directly with more than one Spirit from among the 72. At times, S would "bring" others to talk with us through the board when we had questions that were best answered by them directly. In addition to S, we had direct and lengthy interactions with Astaroth, Furfur, Gremory, Murmur, Focalor, Amy, Camio, and Amdusias. Some of these interactions happened as part of the task that S and Astaroth now said I was actively doing — the task of creating a "New Key." A couple of them, though, happened as we conducted Spirit work with and for other members of our household (like my parents) or our Coven. In either case, these 8 Spirits all came through the board and communicated on their own, giving us an experience of their presence, personality, and voice in a more direct way.

A few other Spirits didn't talk directly to us on the talking board, but still came into very close contact. In these cases, S would bring them close and relay their responses (and something of the personality that came with the Spirit) to us. There were several with whom we interacted this way, but Purson is the one who stands strongest in my memory, even 10 years later.

A small handful of Spirits, S was actively frightened of and advised that we avoid. These Spirits have come to comprise the "Do Not Call" List, and in most cases, S would only give us the scantest of information (if any). When S would speak of them, it was a drain on both S and my partner.

Most of the original working happened in this form of talking board communication, with my then-partner present. However, as my own communication skills strengthened, I improved greatly at hearing S (and other Spirits) more directly. I especially find this to be true when I'm engaged in the writing process — typing, journaling, and editing, in particular. (I tested most of the information I got this way in the beginning by asking again on the board with a partner, having folks do other types of readings for me, or verifying what I could through research. Once I felt confident that I was hearing clearly, I stopped testing as often.) Because of this, some more communication happened and I received more details on my own when I was transcribing the audio recordings and more still when I was writing and editing the original manuscript.

It has been just about 10 years since I first undertook the project of creating this New Key, and though my working partners and techniques have changed somewhat, the Work continues. So what's new for me, and how has it shaped this update and revision?

I work much more independently with the Spirits now than during the first sessions. Then, either my (ex-)wife or Coven were present for all of the talking board communiques. Now, I sometimes have a partner, but I more often don't. I also don't use the board quite as often, and when I do, I'm more likely to utilize a pendulum with it instead of planchette. Because the communication flows so smoothly and quickly at this point, pendulum and "Spirit writing" (discussed in "Methods & Techniques of Spirit Communication" in the Conjurer's Craft section of this book) are now my primary methods for talking with the Spirits.

And I've talked and worked with a lot more Spirits of the Legion — including one from my own "Do Not Call List." (Shocking, I know. I still stand by the need for the List and the warnings I have given. More on that in its own commentary.)

I work with Bael and Paimon regularly now. Monarchs within the Legion certainly pack a punch! I can credit and thank Bael for his role in over-hauling this book/work, in fact — and in helping me see several other writing projects to fruition in the last several months. What an empire builder!

How will I be working with the Spirits of the Lemegeton in 2031 (ten years from this revision)? It's hard to say, except that I am sure I will be involved with them. The better question is: How will YOU be working with them?

On Goetic Magick and Evocation

When we use the phrase "Goetic Magick," what we really mean is sorcery. Some practitioners of the Unseen Arts use the terms Magick and Sorcery interchangeably, but that isn't strictly accurate. Some of our difficulty lies in the imprecise verbiage available to us in English, and other problems in sorting out the differences between the two come from decades (or longer) of writers and teachers conflating the two terms.

Magick might be viewed as a larger scope of ritual, spiritual, and/or energetic practices designed to effect some type of change — either in one's interior world or in the physical world. Depending on the Model of Magick (discussed in the next Commentary) that one employs, a very wide range of techniques, Beings, and energies are available to achieve that desired change.

Sorcery is a subset of Magick that deals specifically with calling upon Spirits and asking for their assistance in the work. Whereas in Magick, a practitioner might raise energy or draw on energies already present, in Sorcery, it is the Spirit who accomplishes the task at hand.

These 72 Spirits are each quite adept at accomplishing different sorts of goals, though you'll find enough overlap between Spirits to be assured of meeting a Spirit with whom you share enough affinity to work in a cordial capacity. I've tried to include enough tables and quick references to make narrowing the field easier.

There is literally no end to the work you can accomplish with the help of "your little daemon." Liberal sciences, necromancy, alchemy, art, foreign language, diplomacy, law, love – these Spirits know all of the things that you want to know. The can make learning significantly easier. They love what you love and will help you pursue, protect, and promote those passions.

So, what does Goetic Magick look like for Witches? Some of that will depend on you and your working tools and methods. You don't have to make it complicated unless that placates your sense of the Arte Magickal. This book offers a complete working system for Witches who are new to working with Spirits and need a starting place — or for Witches who just like to take a peek at other methodologies. However, I don't come to you with the same dire warnings or regimented structures that you find in other Spirit grimoires. You aren't required to do it the way I've described. What I offer is more like guidelines.

Each Spirit is an individual and will have their preferred method of working, it should be noted. Some are chatty, others communicate with images. Some might like complicated ritual and arcane language, while others prefer simplicity. Some sing – all the time. They are as individual and quirky as the Witches and Mages who work with them.

These new descriptions are vital because they give the practitioner an accurate idea of who these Spirits are in the New Aeon. However old the Lemegeton (Ars Goetia, Clavicula Salomonis, etc) may be, we know that the descriptions of the Spirits have persisted in a relatively unchanged state since the 17th Century. Everybody changes at least a little in 400 years, even Spirits. Furthermore, some details weren't recorded accurately in the first place. (As an example, they were all originally described as inherently masculine, regardless of how anciently that Spirit may have been worshipped as a Goddess.)

Communicate with your chosen Spirit in whatever way makes the most sense. If they are verbal, use automatic writing or a talking board as you develop your clairaudient abilities. If they are visual, use a scrying mirror, cauldron, crystal ball, etc. Try trance, flying out, lucid dreaming, smoke/fire scrying; or simply try listening and looking for your Spirit.

The Unseen World is not a separate place, distinct and untouched by This World. Beings of Spirit and beings of flesh walk in both places. We ourselves are, ultimately, beings of Spirit who are also beings of flesh. Spirits know that we inhabit both spaces at once. Mages and Witches should know this, as well.

On Models of Magick

Sorcerers of all ranks and orders tend to approach magick in one of a handful of ways. None is particularly wrong, and none is necessarily right. (Certain approaches can feel uncomfortable or counter-intuitive for certain practitioners, but this doesn't make the model or working system inappropriate. It just means it's a bad fit for that Witch.)

Frater U.D., a German occultist, categorized these "Models/Paradigms of Magick" into five groups. What is helpful about understanding these working models is gaining an appreciation for your own approach, as well as being able to adapt the work of others to suit your own preferred approach. It is from this place that a Spirit Model practitioner like me (and maybe like you), can still find benefit from the writings of occultists working in, for instance, the Psychological Model. It makes the work of others more approachable and adaptable.

Psychological Model

This model is the epitome of Lon Milo DuQuette's saying, "[Magick] is all in your head. You just have no idea how big your head is." This model takes the stance that all magick affects the inner planes, and that daemons, angels, and other Spirits are projections of the Self. This model falls easily in line with Jungian psychology and the exploration of archetypes as projections of the Collective Unconscious. Practitioners working within this model generally have little or no problem with what I have termed "Spirit torture" because, as far as they're concerned, they are whipping some aspect of their own psyches into line. (It could be argued that since they approach the work from this perspective, they are indeed never reaching or impacting Spirits.)

Spirit Model

This model stands in direct contrast to the Psychological Model. Those working within the Spirit Model view daemons, angels, Gods, and Goddesses as distinct and separate individuals with lives and intentions of their own. They are not projections of the Mage or Witch, but exist independently of us. Practitioners working within this model tend to lean toward traditional and folk magick practices, and their worldview tends toward animism and related beliefs.

Energy Model

The Energy Model of magick accepts that something exists outside of the observer, but doesn't claim to know precisely what it is. Like forms of energy that are described by science, Powers in this model tend to be thought of as currents that can be described and categorized (and then utilized) to achieve various goals. In this model, daemons and Godds are similar to elemental, thermodynamic, electromagnetic, or other types of energies. They are forces at work in the Universe that the sciences haven't been able to quantify and define yet.

Information Model

The Information (or Cyber) Model is perhaps the newest paradigm of magick to be described, and it was a concept developed by Frater UD himself based on observation and experimentation. The Cyber Model views the Powers that perform magickal operations as a sort of blank medium upon which the Mage or Witch stamps or feeds an imprint or template. It is the information provided by the operator (practitioner) that programs the Power. This is different than the Energy Model, where Powers are seen as already having a texture, flavor, color, etc, and Powers similar to one's intention are gathered or generated to fuel the work. In the

Information Model, the Power is pure potential, and the Mage gives it texture, color, etc.

Chaos Model

The Chaos Model is sometimes not included with this list — and sometimes it is. It is very much worth including in our discussion, though, since so many Witches are Chaos Mages without realizing it. The Chaos Model says that whatever works is true. Chaos Mages use a liberal mix of all the previous models, sometimes intuitively, and sometimes intentionally. They use whatever works in the moment, whatever method or outlook achieves results.

I operate fairly firmly in the Spirit Model, leaning toward Chaos. Psychological Model is the least resonant for me, and I find it to be in active conflict with the Traditional Witchcraft that I practice. However, when I take stock of my outlook and the rituals and workings I have created, I can see the influence of Energy and Information Models.

I have found that most contemporary Witches operate somewhere on a continuum between Spirit and Chaos. Most pre-modern European Witches (where I draw a lot of inspiration and guidance), also operated on the same continuum — leaning a little more toward Spirit Model than the modern mind.

Our rituals, formulas, and descriptions, then, are written almost entirely from the Spirit Model, which is a departure from modern practice and a return to the roots of Goetic work.

On Evocation, Invocation & Banishing

The earlier edition of this book presupposed a basic magickal education that included a firm understanding and application of Will, grounding, centering, shielding, basic evocation, and banishing techniques. These are the areas of study and practice with which you should be comfortable before attempting to contact Spirits. Any Spirits. This work is an advanced practice (or at least, it is a practice beyond that of the novice).

This edition of the book does not make the same presupposition. In the "Conjurer's Craft" section, you'll find some instruction, formulas, and rituals to aide you in your own development. However, if you find that you want or need more, I might recommend Mat Auryn's *Psychic Witch* or my own *Red Thread Academy: Year 1 Foundations* (which is actually a year-long class). Both resources can be found in the Appendix.

Most editions of the Ars Goetia provide formulas and rituals for evocation, invocation, and banishing of the Spirits. Let's briefly break down what this means.

Evocation — Calling upon the Spirit to be present, outside of the Self

Invocation — Calling upon the Spirit to present, inside the Self. This is often called possession, channeling, aspecting, being ridden, and by many other names.

Banishing — Sending the Spirit away (often forcefully)

In terms of invoking the 72 spirits of the Legion, I simply don't recommend it with any Spirit except your most trusted Familiars. Possessory work is very intimate and involves a great deal of trust, and unless you've been working for a long while with a Spirit and have a particular affinity, you may be asking for trouble. It is not the first approach I'd recommend for getting to know the Spirits.

In regards to evocation, I advocate complete dismissal of previous formulas and rituals in which threats, binding, and torture by fire (or other means) are called upon in order to induce the Spirits to appear before the Mage and do their bidding. If you and the Spirit don't have great enough affinity for each other, or if the Spirit is too mischievous or angry for you to summon without the use of force, you're obviously better off leaving that Spirit alone.

That isn't to say that every Spirit will respond to softly-worded requests. Many of the Legion "require a firm hand and a strong Will" in a Witch/Mage, according to my guides within the Lemegeton. You must be strong, but not abusive or even controlling.

The relationship you are seeking is an old-fashioned one. The Spirits of the Legion refer to Mages and Witches as "Masters," but they are not our slaves. The term "Master" is used with more of the sense of "Master of the Arte." An Adept. Think: Master Mason or Master Carpenter. "Master" of a trade or skill-set, belonging to a guild (which is an erstwhile term for a Coven or "Company"). Not "owner of chattel."

When we enter into relationships with Spirits, they are more like employees, if the relationship stays formal and business-driven; and if we are very lucky, they might become friends. We tend to make contractual agreements with them, whether we realize it or not, for either short or long periods of time. A simple magickal working is relatively short, whereas having a Spirit become your Familiar is quite a long relationship. In either case, you do the Spirit a disservice if you treat them like a slave. They are older than you, often by millennia, and they are probably willing and happy to help you if you treat them decently.

In the event that you have summoned a Spirit who won't leave on their own (and they are causing trouble), you must know how to effectively banish. This next bit of advice should go without saying, but I'll include it anyway out of caution: Don't summon any of the Spirits in this book unless you can also make them go away, if necessary. (As a cautionary note: You really can't force any of the Spirits on the DO NOT CALL list to do anything, including go away – S says, "unless you're Solomon, which you probably aren't." So just refrain from calling them.) We'll cover some banishing techniques in the "Conjurer's Craft" section, in case you don't already have some at your disposal.

My general advice is to be polite, specific, brief, and firm in both your evocations (invitations) and your dismissals (farewells). Forcefully banish only when a Spirit is troublesome for you.

On Spheres and Pyramids

The truest working space of the Sorcerer is not a flat space marked on the ground with words and symbols. Mark the circle and triangle with the names of Godds and Angels (as indicated in most classical grimoires) if it improves your focus, but understand that you live and work in three physical dimensions (and more which aren't of a physical nature).

The Witch needs a Sphere, not a circle, to stand within. She calls Spirits into a Pyramid, not a triangle. Not only do we need to view these forms a little differently, but we need to think of them differently than many contemporary occultists do. Many Mages and Witches view the circle as a place of protection and the triangle as a place of binding or constraint. This, I think you'll find, is not strictly accurate.

Most Witches already work within the multidimensional paradigm, marking their compass in 2D space while visualizing and energizing it in 3D space. Whether or not the ring itself offers protection is actually a matter of debate between Wiccan-derived forms of the Craft and more Traditional ones. I'll leave that point for you to decide based on your own study and experience, but I would suggest you consider the additional function(s) of the "circle" that are known to Trad Crafters.

All Witches, I think, are aware that we are conducting multidimensional operations. The four Elemental Gates form a crossroads, with the World Tree (often represented by a Stang or by the Witch's own person in Trad Craft) at the center. From this central nexus, we travel to ALL planes of existence. In this way, the Compass is a gateway (and is sometimes called a Gateway Ring in folklore).

Additionally, it acts as a vessel — a cauldron of energy when we Tread the Mill. Moreover, it acts as a "wayfinder" (not unlike the vegvisir stave of Iceland) for helping the Powers find their way to us when we perform our rites.

The Pyramid (usually called the "Triangle of Art") is also a multi-dimensional construct, but its purpose is different than the Compass. The Pyramid is a construct that helps give shape and form — physical manifestation — to ethereal Beings. The many Pyramids all over the world are echoes of the concept of the Holy Mountain, where the Godds take flesh and interact bodily with us.

Your triangle on the ground or table, regardless of the material used in its construction, is the footprint for an energetic Pyramid. Within this Pyramid, you offer the Spirits a place to take shape, to interact in a way that one or more of your senses can perceive, and to communicate through the use of divinatory tools.

You can devise your own words for Laying the Compass and Building the Pyramid, or you can use what is provided later in this book. Or use none at all. Rely on Will and vision. Or let the words come extemporaneously from your own sorcery.

On Affinity Between Witch and Spirit

Not every Spirit in the Legion is a good fit for each Witch or Mage. Not only are some Spirits dangerous and should be generally avoided, but many are simply incompatible for a given individual.

A Witch will have a number of potential Spirits from whom they might choose. During the time that the Witch is researching those Spirits, the Spirits might also be observing the Witch.

When a particularly strong attraction presents itself to a Witch, this Spirit is a natural candidate to become a Familiar. Indeed, the Spirit may already be acting in that capacity for the Witch, and the Witch needs only to recognize the Spirit's presence.

Of course, more than one Spirit may be available to you from the Legion, but it is important that you pay close attention to how well these Spirits work with each other before you take on multiple working partnerships with various Spirits. They don't all get along, after all, and to bring too many of them into your life is "to court madness," according to S.

These Spirits, I have found, have friends and allies (and also enemies and enmities) within the Legion. Interestingly, Spirits who are listed next to each other are generally somewhat similar in nature or temperament. Also, Spirits who do similar work tend to get along with each other.

It's more common to have guides and helping Spirits who are under the command of the 72 named Spirits of the Legion than it is to work with multiples of these primary 72, though I've known several people who work happily with multiples.

On Care and Keeping of Familiars

The decision to have a familiar is not a unilateral one. A Witch does not simply choose a Spirit from a list and then trap it within a seal, a bottle, or a figurine. A Familiar is not a spiritual slave or a prisoner.

The relationship between Witch and Familiar Spirit should be mutually beneficial. The Familiar assists in magic, according to their abilities; and the Witch returns energy in the forms of gratitude, gifts, ritual, or something specific to the Familiar. Spirits will often tell you specifically what they want if you just talk to them.

In the section titled "On the Creation of the Legion," I mention that the Spirits don't really care about the metals that have previously been assigned to them. Those metals, and the associated ranks, have planetary alignments (which can be explored in Crowley's *Liber 777*) that can provide some point of reference for the Witch in better understanding the Spirits. However, the correspondences in 777 do not always translate well into the system of Craft you may be practicing, and the Spirits themselves feel ambivalent about the correspondences that Crowley linked to them.

Most familiar Spirits want some sort of housing. This is often a jar or bottle. In the case of my daughter's Familiar, he wanted a little house she had painted for a small plush frog. On the talking board, he said, "I been lookin' at you frog house." He told her he wanted it just as it was – with the acorns spilling out of the door and the cast-off earrings, seashells, and bullet casings still sitting on top. All he asked was that she remove the toy frog's name and add his symbol in its place.

The housing can also take the shape of a candle, statue, or nearly anything physical. My ex-wife's Familiar wanted a black candle as his domain. Mine have wanted a very specific blue sugar bowl, a cane toad "purse," and a tiara. Just ask and they will be very precise, often asking for something you already own.

They almost all like offerings, as well, though the nature of the offerings varies greatly from Spirit to Spirit. Our Coven Familiar wants smoke, and she gave us a specific incense recipe that we were to make and burn for her. The Familiar of one of my students wanted ashes. She didn't care what was burned to create the ash, as long as it was burned with the intention of giving it to the Spirit. Some like honey, mint candies, liquor, or other comestibles. I've never known a Spirit who didn't like blood (anywhere from 1 to 9 drops of your own blood) and whiskey.

I recommend asking your Spirit directly what they want and how often they want it.

On the All and the Adversary

When talking with the Spirits who informed this work, some of them referenced the "All" and the "Adversary." The Spirit "S" had a fair amount to say in those early discussions about these two (especially the All), and others have clarified since then.

Just to be clear, as a Witch and a writer, I am not necessarily advocating for a particular theology or worldview with this commentary. What is expressed here is what was shared with me by the Spirits, and it speaks to how they (at least those who shared) operate. It is a very panentheistic view, in most respects — meaning that Divinity infuses everything. That is different than an animistic view — which purports that everything has a Spirit. Animists don't believe that the same Divine Spirit pervades all things, but that each thing is individual, unique, and en-spirited.

The "All" is the Universal Spirit that penetrates all things (in this panentheistic view, which was relayed by the Spirits of the Legion). It is the totality of existence. The Universe. When Spirits talk of God, this is who/what they mean. Jehovah (JHVH) is a specific and finite being, despite his massive and effective publicity campaign to the contrary. He is part of the All, but the All includes so much more. Jehovah excludes, alienates, and abandons, whereas the All cannot.

JHVH means "I will be what I will be." More commonly, we see this interpreted as "I am that I am." Either way, any one of us could say the same of ourselves. I am, and I will be. So will you. Furthermore, we are also eternal Spirits, creator Spirits. We are like Jehovah, insomuch as the name indicates.

The All is Light, and it is also Dark. Whether you see the Universe in dualities or perceive the many spectrums and continuums, the All covers it and encloses it.

Its opponent is equally real, however. When the Spirits speak of the Shaitan, Satan, the Adversary, they mean a Will or force that is the opposite of All. It is the Great Nothing. It is that which does not have existence. It is Oblivion.

These great forces – which humans know imperfectly and incompletely as God and Satan, under a plethora of names – are not merely myths designed to keep weak-minded, weak-willed sheep enslaved, the Spirits say. They are the great poles of magnetic force in the Universe. Foolish is the Mage (or Witch) who ignores their great Opponent. Careless is the Adept who doesn't recognize their great Ally!

Just as "God" is All, so is the Adversary many. If God is present in all that exists, Satan is present in all that does not. Within science, he is evidenced in black holes and dark matter. He is the absence of being. A pulling apart. An un-doing on a cosmic scale.

Nor is this Force to be confused or conflated with the Folkloric Devil of the Craft. This Great Nothing, this Adversary is not a Light Bringer. "He" brings nothing, not even the Dark. The Adversary is Obliteration. Void.

In the traditional Goetia, the Adversary is called by the name Amaymon, and this force/ideal is served by the most wrathful, violent, and hateful Spirits. These Spirits seek your destruction, just as the Adversary seeks to unmake what is made. These are the Spirits my guides have suggested that nobody call upon.

You'll note, we hope, that Lucifer is not on that list. Not only is Lucifer not included in the 72 spirits of the Goetia, but his name is not synonymous with the Adversary, nor is he his servant. The Light-Bringer is and was a messenger of the All. His "fall from grace" was a willful turning away from a singular focus on the All in order to bring illumination and enlightenment to humanity.

I know that discussion of "God and Satan" is not common in modern magickal texts, particularly in texts intended for Witches.

Most of us believe there is no place for this Adversary in our Craft – that "He" simply doesn't exist. In a very real sense, that is accurate. "That Which Isn't" does not exist. However, there are Spirits and people who serve this Nothing, and therein lies my cautionary note. The Legion believes in the existence of the Adversary, and some do work in the name of this Force.

On the Creation of the Legion

Other writers and magicians more learned and scholarly than I pretend to be have dealt with the historical veracity of the text(s) variously known as "The Lesser Key of Solomon the King," the "Clavicula Salomonis Regis," the "Lemegeton," or the "Ars Goetia." My intention in putting forth this current work is not to disparage or diminish previous scholarship but to add a new voice to the conversation, to shed new light on this old topic.

This information comes, not from the Academic's library, but from the Witch's Sphere and Pyramid. I have talked with several of the 72 spirits in great depth, often enough with other members of my Coven and Tradition. Several of us have Familiar bonds and compacts with specific Spirits among the 72.

Where the creation of the Legion is concerned, most of the information presented here comes directly from Astaroth. (Quite without coincidence, the medieval manuscript that became the Key of Solomon quite clearly states that Astaroth can tell the Mage how the Legion was created and bound.)

Here is what she told us:

> Astaroth is synonymous with Asherah, the Bride of God. Her sacred grove – the famous cedars of Lebanon – were cut down to build Solomon's temple. There were 72 cedars, 72 posts in the temple, 72 Spirits of the Goetia, 72 names of God. The cedars were living sacrifices. Her trees bled for JHVH. Asherah was bound first and forever.

Is this allegorical? Metaphorical? Literal? I'll let you study and judge for yourself.

The following is a mixture of information coming from Astaroth and others of the Legion:

The Spirits of the Legion are of many sorts. Some are truly what we would call demons. Most are something else, though. They are Godds (Bael, Astaroth, Sitri, etc), deceased human Spirits (Samigina, Paimon, etc.), inter-dimensional beings (Purson, Oriax), Djinni, and more. It's as if Solomon took the nearest 72 convenient Spirits – including the Spirit of one of his most beloved wives (herself a Priestess) – and bound them into this grouping in order to accomplish his great work.

As a group, they seem to prefer to be called the "Legion," as opposed to the "Goetia." Only once has my primary guide used the latter term. When asked if we might call up each Spirit in turn, she quickly said NO! "We are the Howling, and to work with us all is to invite madness." Every other time any Spirit has referred to the larger group, they have always said "Legion." Moreover, Astaroth called herself the "Mother of the Legion." (It is my suspicion that this is the general meaning of the term "Lemegeton" — which might otherwise be called a "barbarous word" since it isn't a term from a known, earthly language.)

The distinctions of "King" or "Marquis" or "Duke" and the corresponding metals that are associated with them mean nothing to the Spirits. That information, incidentally, was an editorial addition by Crowley which showed the Spirits supposed planetary alignments. The Spirits themselves don't agree with these associations, per se, and they respond no better to their sigils engraved in their purported planetary metal than they do to their sigils printed or drawn onto paper. (But hey, if inscribing a sigil into the specific metal gives YOU more satisfaction and a deeper sense of your own practice, feel free. Certainly the time and cost to craft such a device imbues it with more of your Will, and it could also be seen as an appropriate offering — of materials, time, skill, and energy.)

Each Spirit rules over a certain number of lesser Spirits – what we might call "egregores" or "familiars" or "Spirit guides." When these lesser Spirits have gained enough strength and power (usually through helping people), they become more like their captains within the Legion. When the "captains" (the 72 named Spirits) gain enough power, they become Godds. They have more freedom and strength, but they will remain bound to the Legion unless the entire body is unleashed (and forgotten) — according to the lore given within the Legion itself.

While a great many Spirits listed in the ranks of the Legion are helpful, others are ambivalent, a few are mischievous, and a handful are servants of the Adversary. These few true demons (these soul eaters, torturers, and murderers of mankind) were included in the Legion very intentionally. The good and the bad are bound together into one unit – Legion – so that Masters afraid of the wickedness of the evil Spirits wouldn't try to unbind the good.

The Spirits are also bound together in the minds of magicians, which binds them together as a unit. As long as we think of them as a group, they will remain a group. Since we can't un-think a thing, they will be bound until humanity forgets about them entirely.

The ranks of the Legion are populated by untold thousands of Spirits who follow ("serve") one of the 72 "captains." These lesser Spirits are of a similar nature to their captains, and often the captains assign one of these others as a Witch's familiar or a person's guide.

On the Meaning and Use of the Seals

The Spirits' seals are somewhat flexible in regards to their form. This is why a few Spirits have more than one seal among the classical texts. These sigils are very much like hieroglyphs or veves, and those who feel drawn to adapting a seal should look to these similar systems of glyphs for inspiration.

Coded into the seals are specific symbol sets that can help Witches and other practitioners better understand the 72 Spirits of the Legion. Below is a listing of the most common symbols and their meanings (as explained by the Spirits themselves) as used within these seals. These should act as guidelines when creating new seals:

3 Dots

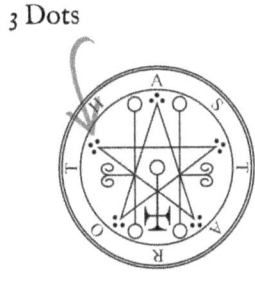

Three dots means a very old Spirit, and there are only two among the Legion who bear that mark (Astaroth and Naberius).

Small Circles

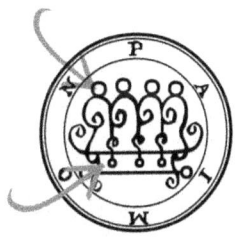

Little circles show realms of influence.

Crosses

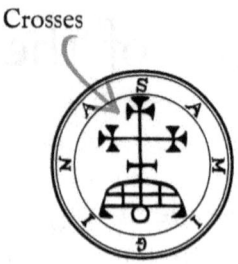

Crosses show good communication. (This includes all lines that cross at right angles, not just Maltese crosses.)

Crescents

Crescents are moons that show "vision power" and wisdom.

Triangles

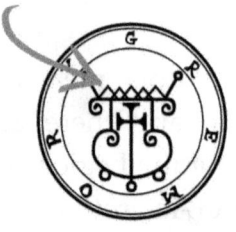

Triangles indicate crowns (high honor and power within the Legion).

S-Lines

Squiggly S lines have to do with the creation of the Spirit itself (ie, used in the creation of the egregore, in cases where that pertains).

The names written in a band around the traditional seals are not required, but they help the Witch with focus and keeping all 72 Spirits straight in one's mind.

Careful consideration of each seal in relation to its Spirit's description will reveal a good deal about the seal's shape and the Spirit's nature.

This work contains alternative seals which can serve as a means of inspiration in creating your own sigils for your Familiar.

You may note that there are no alternate sigils for the Spirits on the DO NOT CALL list. This is a deliberate omission, as my Coven and I didn't want to work directly with these Spirits in order to fashion new and clearer symbols. For us, that would involve evoking those Spirits in order to better understand and represent them.

On Solomon's Ring & Legacy

Some readers of this text will undoubtedly compare our descriptions of the Spirits with older demonologies. Every Spirit description includes passages from these formative works.

One notable omission for the close observer will occur in the case of several Spirits. The older texts will say something like, "The exorcist must hold the magick ring to his face." This comes up especially in the case of Spirits on the DO NOT CALL list. These older versions also include a description of the magick ring (or possibly disc) and how to make it.

This ring (which is sometimes described as a silver or gold finger ring worn on the middle finger of the left hand, and is sometimes described as a silver or gold disc inscribed with three names) is supposed to be a protection against the "foul and flaming breath of these most evil demons." It is also intended to compel them into speaking the truth.

My primary guide from the Legion, however, has stated that such a ring was a special dispensation to Solomon. He was "chosen of JHVH," who had a "Spirit instruct him" in the correct manufacture of the ring for himself. It was a personal tool, and it won't protect anyone but Solomon from Beleth, Asmoday, or the others who seek to undo All.

Indeed, the only way to protect yourself is not to call on Spirits whose aim it is to harm you. Even then, I might add, that I and my Covenmates have had to take special precautions against some of these Spirits. We never called forth any of the Spirits on the DO NOT CALL list, but the fact that such a list is included in this book made us all targets for psychic attack by a few of the nastier demons. They primarily invaded our dreams and caused great psychic and emotional pain until we consciously protected ourselves with our most trusted talismans. The attacks could have been worse, and perhaps unstoppable, if we had directly called them into our space.

On the Greater Legion

Of the surprising pieces of information gleaned while discussing the 72 Spirits of the Legion with our Familiars, one of the most surprising had to be that there are more than 72 Spirits in the Legion. Or, if you will, there is more than one Legion of 72 Spirits.

I haven't delved into this too deeply yet because the current work was large enough without doubling it. To explore 72 (or more) undocumented Spirits seems daunting, though it is a task that I plan to undertake.

Here's what is known (from the guides within the Legion):

The 72 Spirits of the Legion (the ones listed in THIS book, who are sometimes collectively called the Shemhamphorash) were bound together as a unit for a specific magickal working (which has been called "the building of the Great Temple" — though that name may be a metaphor). Under their command are many thousands of lesser Spirits, which is stated rather explicitly in the classical demonologies.

However, other Spirits have been "created" and/or called upon and bound into working "Legions" from one or more separate magickal workings. (Some of these Spirits in the Second and Third Legions are those "lesser Spirits" from the Shemhamphorash, having grown in power enough to become "captains" of their own.)

However they may have come to exist, there is more than one Legion of daemons who are available for Spirit conjuration. Many of the names of these other Spirits are known via history and lore, while others have worked anonymously over the centuries – or haven't worked at all.

Demonic "Do Not Call" List

This is a list of Spirits that you shouldn't summon. This is not an arbitrary list, nor is it based on personal, human opinion. (In fact, there are some listed here that one or more of my Covenmates — and many of my trusted and respected magickal peers — has advocated for.) Our guides within the Legion suggested this list and pointed out specific names for inclusion.

Contrarily, you'll note that there are some questionable, if not outright nasty, Spirits whose names aren't on this list. Only those who "serve the Adversary" (ie, who work toward an "un-making" or annihilation) are listed here. These Spirits, if called into your magickal space, "will lie to you, devise ways to deliver your soul to torture, kill you, or hurt those whom you love. They serve themselves and Oblivion; but they will never serve you, no matter how great your Will nor how much they feign obeisance." So sayeth the trusted Spirit guides who have informed this work.

"To call these is to admit defeat. To call these is to ask to join their service," the trusted Spirits say.

7 Amon

13 Beleth

17 Botis

23 Aim

25 Glasia-Labolas

32 Asmoday

63 Andras

68 Belial

In the decade since this book was originally published, I have been roundly criticized by many ceremonial Magicians for including this list, while simultaneously being lauded by Witches who are grateful for the guidance and plain-dealing. So many practitioners are fearful of interacting with ANY of these 72 Spirits because they know that at least SOME of them are to be avoided. With that intuitive (or even experiential) knowledge and wisdom, most contemporary Witches have steered clear of the whole lot because so many of the Mages with whom they have discourse have been dismissive of their concerns. It has been easier to avoid the entire field, therefore, than it has been to avoid the landmines.

I'll gladly take the criticism and own that the approach and advice that I offer Witches may seem naïve. I suspect this mostly stems from two sources: 1) a lack of understanding about the Models of Magick (or a high value/priority given to the Psychological Model over the Spirit Model), and 2) a certain exuberant confidence on the part of many Mages in their ability to control any Spirit.

While I have known a good number of Ceremonialists who operate at least partially within the Spirit Model, it is safe to make the argument that the vast majority work within the Psychological Model. From that perspective, what is there to fear or avoid in the Legion? Nothing at all! Evoking, commanding, and controlling these "Spirits" is merely an act of calling up one's darker nature to examine, heal, and control it, within that approach. It's just not how most Witches work. (See previous commentary "On Models of Magick.")

The unfortunate outcome of these philosophically opposed Models is that Psychological Model folks often think Spirit Model workers are delusional and superstitious, while Spirit Model workers often see cruelty and hubris in the Psychological Model folks' practices. Education and empathy are the tools that will bridge that gap, I think. In the meantime, my own work is likely to fall into the "delusional and superstitious" category by the majority of Mages. I've made some peace with that, as I recognize that Spirit Model Witches are the audience for whom I write. It is our community who needs these resources — and who will most benefit from the cautionary notes.

There are, of course, some Spirit Model operators who object to my inclusion of these eight names on this list. Of these, the largest proportion believe they (and perhaps a select group of others) are strong enough, knowledgeable enough, or are in some other way uniquely gifted or marked, such that they will not be adversely affected by one or more of these eight Spirits.

Honestly, I don't feel it's my place to pass judgment on those insights and beliefs. Perhaps they are, and are more intrepid than I am. Perhaps they aren't special/strong/wise enough to be safe, and have been lulled into ruinous hubris.

Furthermore, I recognize that no warning I give could be dire enough to dissuade a practitioner who is determined to try. The warning given here against working with these few Spirits is based on adamant advice from trusted counselors within the Legion. I offer it sincerely and with humility to my fellow Witches, hoping only that you'll consider it deeply and seriously.

Goetic Correspondences

Creating a usable Table of Correspondences is no easy task where the Legion is concerned. As I have been told by several Spirits within the Legion, not all Spirits have a sign, planet, element, or direction with which they are associated. Most have at least one of these associations, and a rare few have all of them. However, to create a table in which every cell is full would require force, and it would ultimately be inauthentic for the contemporary Witch.

The information that follows is partially taken from the original texts and partially derived from talking board and pendulum conversations with the Guides. Take the following information, then, for what you will. It is meant to help you find the Spirits who can best assist you. It is not meant to be a definitive compendium. Feel free to dig deeper and seek out your own associations and understandings.

Furthermore, as mentioned elsewhere, the tables in Crowley's *Liber 777* (which associate the Spirits of the Legion with astrological decans – and, by extension, with the classical planets, elements, directions, Tarot cards, metals, incenses, and more) can be useful to the Mage who feels inclined toward that system. There is an egregore surrounding that system that has gathered energy since at least the time of its first publishing in 1909. (Since it was extrapolated and revised from an earlier Golden Dawn text, the egregore has been living and working within the magical community for many years prior to that, as well).

What is offered here is simpler, more direct, and will (in some cases) conflict with *Liber 777*.

Details are not provided for the eight Spirits on the "Do Not Call" list.

Goetic Correspondences

	Spirit	Sign	Planet	Element	Direction
1	Bael		Mercury		
2	Agares		Mars		
3	Vassago		Moon	Water	
4	Samigina				
5	Marbas	Leo	Mercury		
6	Valefor				
7	Amon				
8	Barbatos	Sagittarius	Jupiter		
9	Paimon		Venus		West
10	Buer	Sagittarius			
11	Gusion				
12	Sitri	Aquarius	Venus	Water	
13	Beleth				
14	Leraje	Sagittarius			
15	Eligos		Mars		
16	Zepar		Mars		
17	Botis				
18	Bathin		Moon		
19	Sallos		Mars		

Goetic Correspondences

	Spirit	Sign	Planet	Element	Direction
20	Purson		Mercury		
21	Marax	Taurus			
22	Ipos	Leo			
23	Aim				
24	Nebarius				
25	Glasya-Labolas				
26	Bune		Saturn		
27	Ronove				
28	Berith	Aries			
29	Astaroth	Virgo, Libra	Venus		West
30	Forneus			Water	
31	Foras			Water	
32	Asmoday				
33	Gaap	Scorpio, Leo, Taurus, Aquarius			South
34	Furfur			Fire	
35	Marchosias				
36	Stolas				
37	Phenex	Leo, Scorpio	Sun	Fire	

Goetic Correspondences

	Spirit	Sign	Planet	Element	Direction
38	Halphas		Mars		
39	Malphas		Mars		
40	Raum				
41	Focalor			Water	
42	Vepar	Libra	Venus	Water	West
43	Sabnock	Aries, Leo	Mars		
44	Shax		Venus		
45	Vine	Gemini			
46	Bifrons	Gemini			
47	Uvall			Air	
48	Haagenti				
49	Crocell	Cancer	Saturn	Water	
50	Furcas				
51	Balam				
52	Alloces	Leo	Mars	Fire	
53	Camio		Jupiter	Air	
54	Murmur		Moon	Water	
55	Orobas				
56	Gremory	Cancer	Venus	Water	
57	Ose		Mercury		East

Goetic Correspondences

	Spirit	Sign	Planet	Element	Direction
58	Amy			Fire	
59	Oriax	Leo			
60	Vapula	Cancer, Virgo, Libra, Pisces	Venus	Water	
61	Zagan				
62	Valak			Earth	
63	Andras				
64	Haures		Sun	Fire	East
65	Andrealphus				
66	Kamaris				South
67	Admusias				
68	Belial				
69	Decarabia	Virgo, Capricorn	Venus	Water	East
70	Seere				
71	Dantalion				
72	Andromalius	Libra			

Areas of Influence & Interest

The following quick reference is intended to help you find those Spirits who are skilled in the areas in which you need assistance or have an interest. Please do not rely solely on this list, but instead use it as a way to narrow the field. The Spirit descriptions that follow will be much more informative regarding the specific manner in which each Spirit can help you with the topics and skills listed below.

As with other lists and charts in this book, the eight Spirits on the "Do Not Call" List are not included here. However, you'll find this chart extremely helpful in determining an alternate Spirit to call to help you with any skill or power conferred by those eight.

Areas of Influence & Interest

Alchemy, Transmutation, Transformation	5. Marbas
	28. Haagenti
	59. Oriax
	61. Zagan
Animal Communication	8. Barbatos
	53. Camio
	69. Decarabia
Astral Travel, Spirit Journey, Witch Flight	33. Gaap
Astronomy, Astrology, Star Lore	21. Marax
	36. Stolas
	50. Furcas
	52. Alloces
	58. Amy
	59. Oriax
	65. Andrealphus
Athletics	2. Agares
Competition	14. Leraje
Destruction	40. Raum
	41. Focalor
	43. Sabnock
	64. Haures

Areas of Influence & Interest

Discord, Strife, Conflict	17. Botis
Disease, Wounds (inflicting)	42. Vepar
	43. Sabnock
	64. Haures
Divination, Scrying, Visions	3. Vassago
	5. Marbas
	8. Barbatos
	9. Paimon
	11. Gusion
	15. Eligos
	17. Botis
	20. Purson
	21. Marax
	22. Ipos
	26. Bune
	28. Berith
	29. Astaroth
	30. Forneus
	33. Gaap
	34. Furfur

Areas of Influence & Interest

	40. Raum
	45. Vine
	47. Uvall
	53. Camio
	54. Murmur
	56. Gremory
	57. Ose
	64. Haures
	69. Decarabia
Energy Movement	62. Valak
Friendship, Alliances	47. Uvall
	55. Orabos
Geometry (and all Mathematics)	46. Bifrons
	49. Crocell
	65. Andrealphus
Giving Good Familiars	6. Valefor
	10. Buer
	20. Purson
	21. Marax
	27. Ronove

Areas of Influence & Interest

	36. Stolas
	43. Sabnock
	44. Shax
	51. Alloces
	67. Amdusias
Languages	2. Agares
	27. Ronove
Law, Ethics, Justice	24. Nebarius
	53. Camio
	72. Andromalius
Liberal Arts (all)	9. Paimon
	24. Nebarious
	25. Astaroth
	46. Bifrons
	71. Dantalion
Liberal Sciences (all)	4. Samigina
	9. Paimon
	21. Marax
	24. Nebarius
	29. Astaroth

Areas of Influence & Interest

	33. Gaap
	37. Phenex
	46. Bifrons
	49. Crocell
	50. Furcas
	51. Balam
	52. Alloces
	57. Ose
	58. Amy
	60. Vapula
	71. Dantalion
Logic	10. Buer
	31. Foras
	50. Furcas
	66. Kamaris
Love, Lust, Sex	9. Paimon
	12. Sitri
	15. Eligos
	19. Sallos
	34. Furfur

Areas of Influence & Interest

	40. Raum
	44. Shax
	47. Uvall
	60. Vapula
Mechanical Arts, Building, Engineering	5. Marbas
Medicine, Healing	5. Marbas
	10. Buer
Money	40. Raum
	44. Shax
Music, Singing, Poetry	9. Paimon
	42. Vepar
	67. Amdusias
Mysteries, Hidden Things, Secrets, Occult Lore	5. Marbas
	8. Barbatos
	15. Eligos
	20. Purson
	29. Astaroth
	30. Forneus
	37. Phenex
	44. Shax

Areas of Influence & Interest

	45. Vine
	55. Orobas
	56. Gremory
	64. Haures
	66. Kamaris
	71. Dantalion
	72. Andromalius
Necromancy, Ancestor Work	4. Samigina
	26. Bune
	46. Bifrons
	54. Murmur
Philosophy	10. Buer
	33. Gaap
	50. Furcas
	54. Murmur
	60. Vapula
Plant Lore, Herbs, Woods	8. Barbatos
	10. Buer
	18. Bathin
	21. Marax

Areas of Influence & Interest

	31. Foras
	36. Stolas
	46. Bifrons
Reputation, Dignity, Praise, Honors, Awards	55. Orabos
	59. Oriax
Rhetoric, Communication, Debate	11. Gusion
	24. Nebarius
	26. Bune
	27. Ronove
	31. Foras
	50. Furcas
	53. Camio
	66. Kamaris
Shapeshifting, Fetch Work	1. Bael
	57. Ose
	65. Andrealphus
Sleight of Hand, Illusion	6. Valefor
Speaking in Tongues	30. Forneus
Stone Lore	8. Barbatos
	18. Bathin

Areas of Influence & Interest

	21. Marax
	31. Foras
	36. Stolas
	46. Bifrons
	69. Decarabia
Tree Lore and Communication	8. Barbatos
	67. Amdusias
War, Strategy, Defense	15. Eligos
	16. Zepar
	19. Sallos
	38. Halphas
	39. Malphas
	43. Sabnock
Water, Sea, Sailing	41. Focalor
	42. Vepar
	49. Crocell
Weather Magick	34. Furfur
	41. Focalor
	42. Vepar
Witchcraft	10. Buer
	18. Bathin

The Conjurer's Craft

Each of the discussions and liturgical pieces in this section are intended to provide a blueprint or starting point for the Witch who wishes to connect with one or more Goetic Spirits. They are presented in roughly the order of service for a ritual. Together they form a complete Goetic rite for Witches.

We begin by establishing which of the Witch's tools will be most needed for Goetic workings, and then we discuss each of the ritual elements. Liturgical and formulary pieces are included on pages with a graphic border. These liturgical selections can be adapted or used as they are.

Order Of Service

    Align the Three Souls

    Cleanse the Space and the Self

    Lay the Compass and Build the Pyramid

    Invitation to Chosen Spirit

    Knowledge and Conversation

    Making the Compact

    Red Meal

    Farewell to Chosen Spirit

    End

The entire process is fairly straightforward, if you are already experienced as a ritualist. If you are less experienced, the cadence of the working should still feel fairly intuitive. In short, we do a little tidying and personal check-in to prep for our guest; invite and receive said guest; talk about the topics under consideration; negotiate a bargain in both parties' interests; share a meal; and then say goodbye.

Absolutely any and every piece of ritual shared here is adaptable. I'm not the sort of Witch who says, "You must perform the ritual as I've written it, otherwise you invite failure and destruction." What rubbish! Rituals as written typically work best for the Witch or Mage who did the writing. They reflect that practitioner's sense of the Arte and the guidance of their own Familiar Spirit. If you feel comfortable in your understanding of any given peace, by all means, do what you must to make it yours.

Tools of Conjuration

You may have a large complement of ritual implements for your Witchcraft practice, many of which will be specific to your Tradition or to your skills and proclivities. As a part of your Spirit conjuration practice, you could theoretically employ all of them, if you feel so inclined. Witchcraft has the potential for endless creativity and adaptation.

Because we could find a theoretical use for every Witch tool, it is more fruitful and efficient to focus instead on only those tools that will be utilized in the ritual components shared in this book. This list, therefore, will be fairly small, specific, and in no way exhaustive. It is a starting place, like everything in this grimoire.

Hooded Robe

Come to the Millgrounds (the area where you cast your circle or lay your Compass) wearing either black robes with a hood or veil or in some other specially designated garb with an attached or separate head covering.

You want to be comfortable and unrestricted in your movements, and the garments you wear should be clean. The hood or veil will serve the purpose of helping to eliminate visual distractions from your periphery, as well as being handy for blocking all visual stimulus during seething.

With my own robes, I keep a linen sachet of frankincense, lavender, and vervain. You can lay your robe, veil, and sachet in a drawer or trunk for safekeeping between workings, or tie the sachet with a loop of ribbon to dangle from the same hanger as your robe in a closet. These herbs are associated with cleansing, protection, and Craft power.

Rope and Feathers

The Witch's ladder can take many forms and serve a myriad of purposes. One of the oldest forms is that of the rope and feathers. In this version, a rope, string, or ribbon is knotted to store a spell. Feathers (or charms, stones, etc) are either tied into knots as they are made, or they are braided or twisted into the cord or rope as it is formed.

In our case, we would create a ladder of protection which could then be unknotted if needed to release its power. We'll talk more about using this cord in the discussion entitled "In Case of Emergency" at the end of this section.

One method of creating your own rope and feathers for protection during Goetic workings is shared in the resources following this discussion.

Stang

Many Trad Crafters work with a Stang, which in its simplest form is a forked stick of about staff height. The liturgy in this grimoire for Laying the Compass calls for a Stang, and the Stang acts as a palpable reminder of the Witch Father in his guise as Auld Hornie — as well as the Witch Mother, the Weaver who works her distaff.

If you don't have or use a Stang, a staff can serve the purpose to the extent of Laying the Compass. Likewise, if you have another preferred method of building thieWitch's Sphere, you might leave the Stang out all together.

I can recommend several types of Stang to the Witch who would like to make, purchase, or adapt one. The first, of course, is a forked branch harvested from a living and willing tree. Be sure to give the tree an offering. Three or nine drops of your own blood being quite traditional.

You might also purchase a ready-made Stang from a witchy artisan, like my friend Paul at Artes and Craft who made mine. Purchased Stangs often feature poles that have been stripped of their bark and polished and sealed with linseed oil (or similar) and topped with either metal horns or animal horns/antlers. Goat horns and stag antlers being the most common. (See Appendix B for suppliers of Stangs.)

You might choose to craft your own Stang by topping a staff with horns. Deer antlers still connected by a bit of skull for mounting are relatively easy to find online and at local flea markets. A few witchy suppliers also offer Stang toppers. (See Appendix B.)

Finally, you can repurpose a hay fork or pitchfork for your own Stang. Either two or three tines are traditional, to emulate the horned one and the distaff, so you may need to use metalworking tools to remove superfluous tines.

In all cases, the Witch should "shoe" the Stang themselves in a ceremonial setting. This is the final step, which activates and consecrates the Stang for use. Shoe your Stang when the moon is waxing or full. Use the Saining Ritual provided at the end of this chapter for the Stang and all other tools. Shoe the Stang with either an iron nail (like a coffin nail) or a metal butt cap.

To erect the Stang in the middle of the Compass or at one of the directional gates, I recommend a cast iron umbrella stand like the ones used for patio umbrellas.

Black, White, and Red Handled Knives

Earlier versions of the *Ars Goetia* are very specific about the shape, markings, and materials of the black and white knives, called the athame and kerfane/bolline respectively. They are silent on the red knife, as such, but knives like it exist in many classical texts without mention of color, materials, or inscriptions. All three knives are included here, as all are needful in Witchcraft conjurations.

The athame is a black-handled knife upon which certain markings are traditionally made. These markings help empower the blade and activate it for the cutting and describing of spiritual energy. Typically a black-handled blade is used only to cut on the etheric plane, and it needn't be physically very sharp to do this. (I like a sharp Black Knife, personally.)

The white-handled knife is classically depicted as being roughly the same size and shape as the black-handled blade. The differences between them lie more in their hilt colors, inscriptions, and purposes than in their hilt-shape or blade style. Many contemporary Witches like a sickle (called a bolline), but this is a very specific type of tool. This blade is almost solely used for harvesting herbs and cutting ritual cords. A kerfane-style white-handled knife, though, can cut anything physical, except flesh. Like the athame, its traditional markings empower it to its purpose.

The red handled knife, often called a lancet, thumb-pricker, or shelg, is a bloodletting tool. No classical inscriptions exist for this blade but I suggest the following:

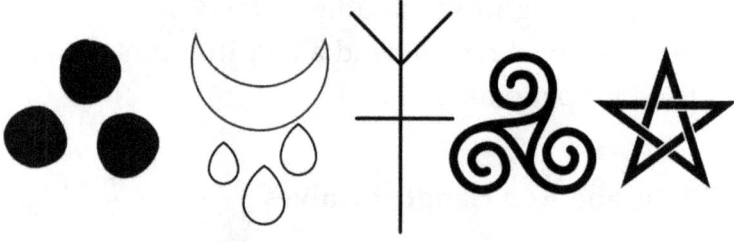

The following two pages show classic illustrations for the Solomonic blades and their corresponding inscriptions.

PLATE XIII.

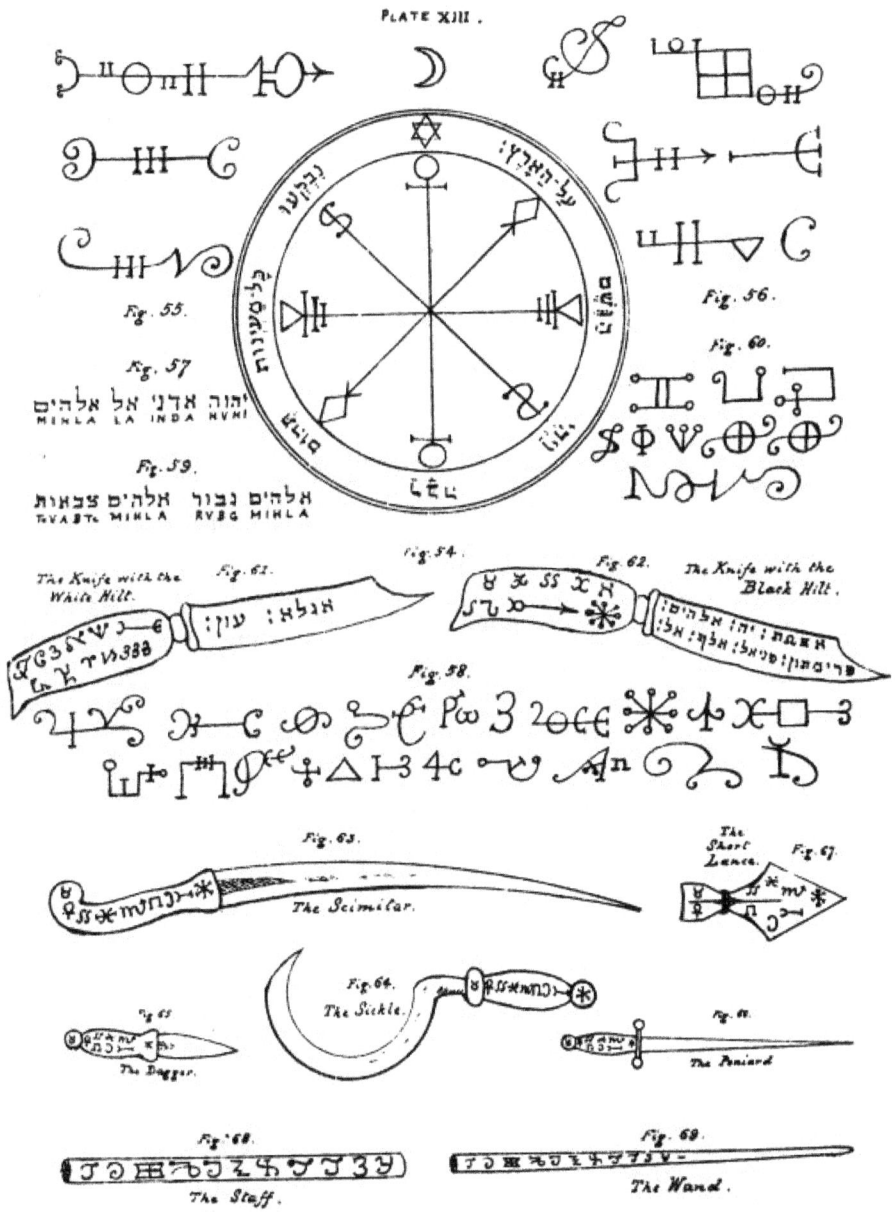

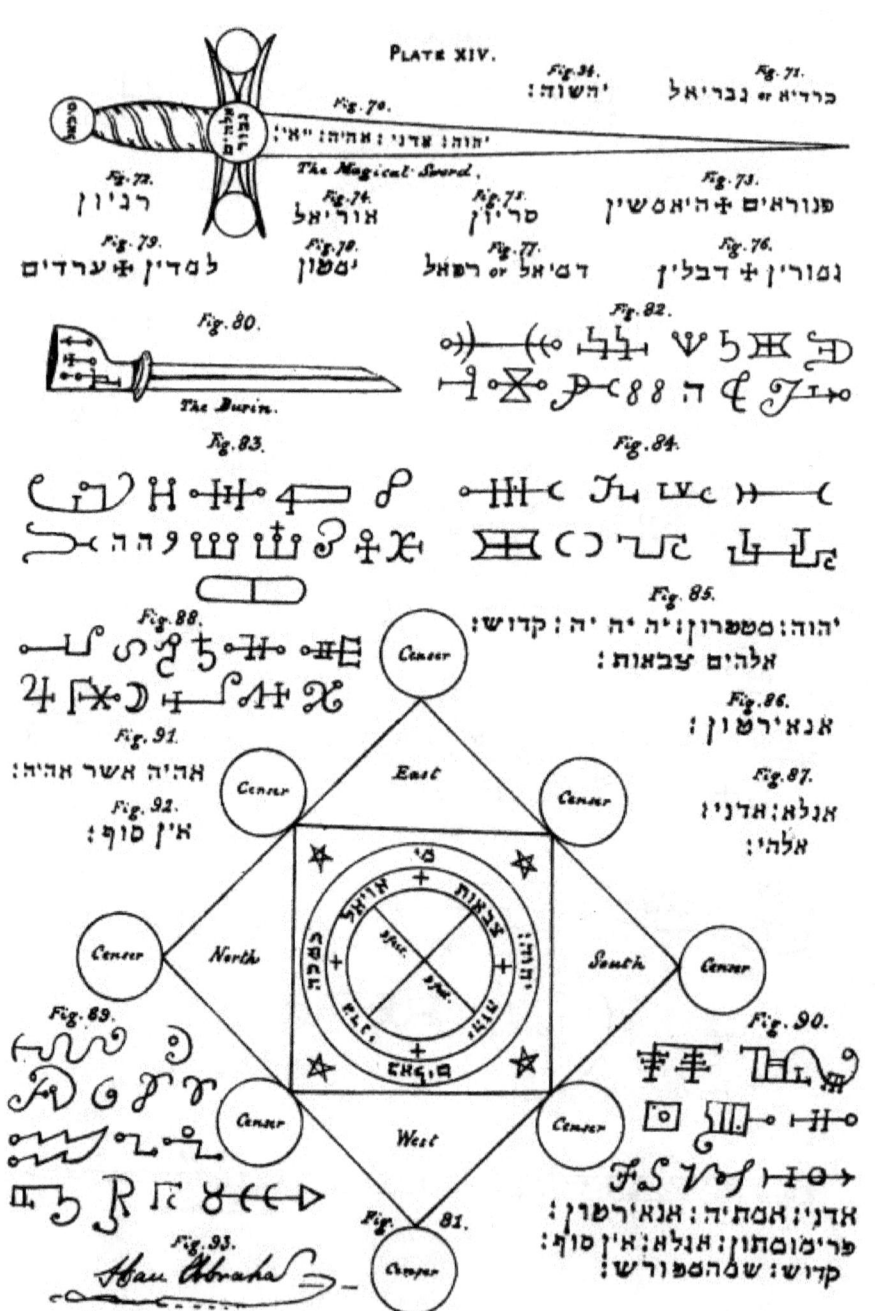

Many Crafters use the black-handled athame as an evocation tool. I can't discourage this in strong enough terms. An evocation is a calling forth. An invitation. Inviting a guest to a conversation or dinner at the point of a knife speaks more of coercion than hospitality. At the very least, the threat is implied, like keeping a pistol on the table during a chat.

The purpose of this instrument is twofold: energetic carving / inscription tool, and spiritual weapon. As a carving / cutting tool of energy, you might use it to sever a link, mark an area or object on the Unseen level, or cut off a disruptive energy in the vicinity (not unlike cutting a storm in order to divert it). As a weapon, you might brandish it at an Unseen threat or wield it with the intent to deflect an attack, or even to harm the attacker.

The white-handled knife is purely functional in the physical realm. Use it for any cutting or carving needs while you do magick and ritual. You will undoubtedly need to carve a candle, chop an herb, or cut a cord at some point. Keep your White Knife handy and sharp enough to handle these tasks.

You'll want a razor sharp edge or point on your red-handled knife. Blood offering of one, three, five, or nine drops of your own blood is a traditional offering in exchange for help from the Unseen. Other offerings exist, which we will discuss soon under its own heading, but blood is pretty much always happily accepted. That's because it is an offering of our own vital essence. Our lives and our energetic signatures are carried on this tide. Oaths made on our blood seal our vital nature to the keeping of the promise. For those times when you find it needful to make oath or offering, keep your Red Knife (which can be designed either to poke or to slice) clean, sharp, and at the ready.

When you get a new knife, be sure to sain it, using the ritual included in this book or one of your own devising.

Sigils

The sigils or seals of the Spirit whom you are contacting are used to aid your focus and to specify which Spirit you are evoking. Think of these sigils as calling cards. The visual imagery embedded within the sigil, especially when combined with the Spirit's name, assist you in dialing in to their power and presence.

I've mentioned elsewhere that these sigils do not have to be crafted from specific metals, as directed in Aleister Crowley's work on the *Ars Goetia* and in *Liber 777*. Goetic sorcerers worked with these symbols, and certainly with the Spirits, long before Crowley created his table of correspondences.

To that end, you may decide that you want to adapt or create your own table of correspondences, inclusive of these Spirits — tables aligned with your own elemental, planetary, or other associations as appropriate to the Craft you practice. Such a table would be much more useful for many Witches, as it would reduce the amount of cognitive dissonance that often happens for us when we try to align our individual or Tradition's cosmology with that of others. For example, if you practice within a system that places Air in the North (not in the east as in ceremonial Magic), Earth in the South (not North), and Fire in the East (not South), you can see how Ceremonial Magick tables already need to shift for your use.

Another option, and one I particularly advocate, is to let the Spirits tell you their preferences. You may not be concerned with the desires and alignments of all 72 Spirits. Your focus may be only on the one or few or several with whom you are developing a working relationship. Narrowing your focus, of course, means that you won't have nice, neat categories and subcategories that can be ultra-satisfying in a chart or table (if you like that sort of thing, which some of us really do), but it does help you prioritize your own energy and get to know the Spirits as individuals with their own stories, aspirations, desires, and the like.

Of course, one consideration with this personal approach is that you'll only have other people's descriptions, mine included, of a Spirit to start with. If no mention is made of preferred materials, what material do you use to make a sigil to initiate contact?

Paper works. Draw the sigil onto paper, wood, cotton broadcloth, or some other simple base. Don't overthink it. If the Spirit has a preference, trust that they will let you know.

The last consideration to discuss in producing physical seals is to accommodate your own sense of the Arte. If a free-handed sigil on computer paper seems sloppy or unprepared to you, as it does for some people, you'll want to invest some time, attention, and maybe even money in crafting seals that will please you. Maybe pyrography (wood burning), etching, engraving, embroidery, or painting will satisfy your sense of style and fulfill your need to engage in the ritual of preparation.

Pyramid

The actual Pyramid you build, like your sphere/compass, is energetically constructed in multiple dimensions — the three dimensions of our physical, consensus reality, plus those involved in spiritual and energetic realities. It is marked, however, by a rather two-dimensional triangle in this world.

Both the Sphere and the Pyramid can actually be marked this way, in fact. The Compass Laying ritual included later in this book isn't designed with a material marker on the floor/ground, but it could be adapted if that is your preference. Round rugs and circular tapestries provide an ideal surface for painting or embroidering a reusable and movable Sphere. Just flip the rug over and use the stiff, blank underside as your canvas. Or utilize colored sand, cornstarch, cording, twigs, or stones to lay the boundary markings.

Traditional "Triangles of Art" are marked with names and

words of protection and manifestation. If you like, you can make something similar, incorporating names and words of power from your Tradition.

Here are three examples.

This is the traditional triangle included in Solomonic grimoires.

This triangle has been adapted into a specifically Thelemic paradigm.

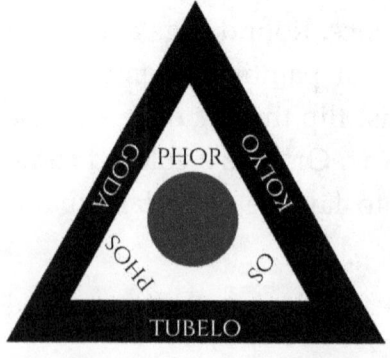

This final one is adapted for use in my own Craft Tradition — the Spiral Castle Tradition, part of American Folkloric Witchcraft.

The Pyramid can be marked very simply, though, if that is your preference. Three twigs or branches of equal length, laid upon the ground/floor work beautifully.

However you craft your Pyramid, it should be large enough for you to place inside it a scrying bowl or mirror — or pendulum mat, talking board, or other communication tool. The same principle applies to your Sphere. It should be at least large enough for you to sit cross-legged in its center — and ideally to lie down. Nine feet in diameter is traditional, but I've seen lots of 3-ft and 6-ft diameter circles in practice.

Scrying Tools

We're going to talk about "Methods and Techniques of Spirit Communication" later in this grimoire, but as you're preparing and gathering your Conjurer's tool chest, we ought to mention some of the more common communication tools here. You'll want at least one of these and possibly several, depending on the style and communication methods preferred by you and your Spirits.

The *crystal ball* is a classic tool of Spirit conjuration and communication. It provides a temporary vessel that Spirits often enjoy. Also, this medium is often quite accessible for scryers to seek images in. I tend to favor clear quartz crystal over lead crystal — which is essentially fancy glass in which the maker substituted lead oxide for the more standard calcium, giving the finished product a refractive, rainbow-inducing quality. I favor the quartz crystal because it is a naturally occurring substance that is often enhanced by occlusions, markings, and other unique features within the orb, thus making some aspects of scrying easier. The properties of the stone itself, of course, are well documented, and it has long been praised for its energy conducting and visionary qualities.

All that being said, a lead crystal or other glass ball can work nicely for many Witches. This is especially true if you have an emotional or sentimental link with the ball. I have a lead crystal ball that belonged to my grandfather and to his grandmother before that. My great-great-grandmother used it as a paperweight, I am told, but my grandfather (who was deeply interested in visionary and Spirit work) actually used it for scrying. This ball has always worked very well for me, as have some other glass and lead crystal pieces.

Both *light mirrors* (standard-style mirrors, usually backed with

SCRYING CRYSTALS -- QUARTZ CRYSTAL SKULL, LARGE QUARTZ POINT, GLASS APPLE, LEAD CRYSTAL BALL, QUARTZ CRYSTAL BALL, GLASS DOORKNOB

polished metal or a light-colored reflective foil) and *dark mirrors* (glass painted black on one side — or carved and polished from a black stone like obsidian) are great choices. Neither is particularly hard to purchase online or in specialty stores. And the dark mirror can even be crafted by the Witch, an act of preparation that can lend great power. (Find instructions for this at the end of this chapter.) When selecting or making such a mirror, choose one in which your whole face is visible, as this will aid in the visionary experience.

LIGHT AND DARK MIRRORS

Scrying into a water filled *bowl* or *cauldron* is very effective and has ancient roots. It harkens to gazing into sacred pools and wells, so many of which have connections to prophecy and Spirit lore.

Typically, either a black glass or stone bowl is used, but some practitioners prefer a crystal bowl. In fact, Ted Andrews' <u>Crystal Balls and Crystal Bowls</u> is one of the instruction books I often recommend to those new to the art of scrying.

Almost all bowls currently being marketed as scrying bowls are black stone, but some are simple black ceramic. However, beautiful bowls of lead crystal or semi-precious stone in every color could be employed, if they speak to the Seer.

Some Witches prefer to keep one or two non-visionary communication tools on hand, either because they like the variety, aren't particularly visual themselves, have a condition called aphantasia in which they can't visualize things that aren't physically present, or because they know that some Spirits aren't visual communicators. Of the tools to keep on hand in any of these cases, the talking board and pendulum are the most common.

The *talking board*, in particular, is a very verbal way of communicating, and it can be ideal for Witches or Spirits who like to talk, hear, or write. It can be used alone or with a partner or small group. My preference has always been for partnered work on a talking board, as I enjoy the energy boost of using it with another Witch. However, sometimes the energies of three or more practitioners can diffuse the focus and usefulness of the tool, in my experience.

Pendulums are exceptionally useful for the solo practitioner who wants a more verbal type of experience, as well. The pendulum is always a single-operator tool, and it is adaptable in its complexity of use and communication. A very simple pendulum session can involve just a plumb or heavy pendant on a string and a series of "yes/no" questions. A more complicated setup might involve a fancier plumb and cording, a pendulum mat, and maybe even a stand fitted for the pendulum to offer a hands-free experience.

Pendulum mats can be marked with a "yes/no" chart, but they often feature a semi-circle of letters and numbers, and sometimes symbols like the zodiacal, elemental, and planetary glyphs. Cloth,

TALKING BOARD, PLANCHETTE, PENDULUMS, PENDULUM MAT

leather, and wood are the most common base materials for these mats.

Consumables

There are a few "tools" that you will consume as part of your workings. These include:

Candles/lanterns and accoutrement

Incense and accoutrement

Housle accoutrement

There are ways to dive deep on your preparation of each of these items. **Candles, lanterns, or oil lamps** can be ritually created and blessed to become Lamps of Arte. My own method of Creating Lamps of Arte is shared at the end of this chapter. Or conversely, a Witch might use very straightforward and utilitarian means of illumination — 1 to 4 candles in holders. Either way, some means of lighting should be considered and accounted for.

I recommend three *incenses* to be used by the Conjurer - the first for purification, the second for invitations/evocation, and the final for banishing (in extreme need). I prefer loose incense, as this is the most direct method of crafting your own. It can be sprinkled onto charcoal tablets in an incense bowl or thurible or tossed onto embers in a fire. The three recipes that follow are what I use in this work unless a Spirit has given me their preferred recipe for the invitation.

The *Housle (or Red Meal)* is part of the offering in a working, and will be treated on in more detail in the "Offerings" later in this Conjurer's Craft section. The tools of the Housle are an offering bowl or lipped dish, a cup, and a sacrificial Red Knife.

Blessed waters, including what we would contemporarily consider perfumes, have a long association with Spirit work. Most

Witches ready to start a Goetic practice will already have a method of blessing or consecrating water. However if you don't yet or if you are open to trying something new, I'd like to suggest preparing what the ancient Greeks called *khernips*.

This simple form of holy water, by the way, isn't reliant on the Witch's or Mage's inherent power to activate it and make it holy. Rather these items are considered inherently pure and could be viewed from a traditional perspective as being inspirited. Bringing them together creates a powerful agent for cleansing oneself and the ritual space.

A variety of scented "waters" come to us from the Middle ages and beyond, and the botanicals used to scent them are specifically associated with either calling upon beneficent Spirits or driving out malevolent ones. The use of these perfumes has been handed down in various traditions and practices — often without the practitioners knowing or understanding why they work. My own High Priestess, for example, taught our Coven to use perfume at the end of possessory work, particularly if the Spirit wasn't leaving the body easily. For her, any floral perfume would work. It was applied to the back of the neck, the palms, the brow, and the soles of the feet.

I find that I like two formulas best for this. The first is Murray and Lanman's classic *eau de toilette* Florida Water, which is a staple in Hoodoo and American Voudon for just the type of work we are discussing — cleansing and clearing after Spirit work. You can purchase Florida Water from grocery stores, pharmacies, and online retailers.

Or you can blend my other favorite water — "Venus Water." The components of Venus Water (which is also called Angel Water), are associated with love, passion, beauty, and enlightenment, as are the beings most associated with the corresponding planetary body. Venus is the light-bringer, and the myths and lore that come to us are of sojourns and trials in the Underworld and enchantment and sorcery in the Green World. Both the Witch Father and Witch Mother have associations with the planet Venus, making Venus Water an ideal choice for crafters.

Saining of Tools

It is customary when a Witch acquires new tools to cleanse and consecrate them to their own use. This is true whether the tools are purchased, homemade, or received as a gift, and also whether they are for personal or coven use.

The term "sain" is an archaic word that means to make the sign of the cross over something in order to banish evil or unwanted forces from it, or viewed another way, to bless it so that evil cannot touch it. The symbol of the cross as a sign of blessing far pre-dates Christianity. Indeed, the equal-armed cross (often depicted with a circle encompassing it) is a prehistoric and universal symbol of which every land and culture had some version. It is a symbol that is related to concepts of perfection and the totality of known existence.

Materials:
> the tool to be sained
> dark bread in a bowl (or lipped dish)
> red wine in a cup
> the Red Knife
> a lancet (optional)
> a portion of purification or blessing incense
> a thurible with a lit charcoal

1.) Lay the Compass, as usual.

2.) Place some of the incense on the lit charcoal and run the tool through the resulting smoke making the shape of a cross, visualizing all past energies of the tool being carried away and dissolved with the smoke.

3.) Say: "I cleanse this '[*tool*]' in the name of the Mighty Ones, that it may serve me well in my Craft."

4.) Raise power by seething. Rock back and forth, hum, chant, wail, and draw power up from the third realm and down from the first realm into yourself and into your tool.

5.) Perform the rite of the Housle.

6.) Anoint the tool with a cross of the sacrificial fluid, giving it a name at this time if you so wish. The Housle is the blood of the Mighty Ones.

7.) Finally, raise a drop of your own blood for the third and final cross in the Saining.

Preparing the Rope and Feathers

Usually, you would prepare this item in advance, as it can take hours of braiding and an outlay of energy.

Materials

9 yd of ribbon or cording

9 feathers or charms

White handled knife or scissors

Timing

Gather the materials and perform your spell on a Wednesday night during the Full Moon. If possible, time your Laying the Compass to coincide with "Jupiter hour," which will begin approximately 3 hours after sunset.

Process

1. Lay the Compass in your usual fashion, or use the method provided in this grimoire.

2. Say the following aloud three times as you hold the cording and feathers in your hands: "*I call upon the Ancient Powers. By the might of three times three, let harm and hurt pass over me.*"

3. Say one of the following strings of barbarous words that come to us from the Greek Magical Papyri: (to call the Witch Mother's power) PHORBA PHORBOBAR BARO PHORPHOR PHORBAI; (to call the Witch Father's power) ABRAT ABRASAX SESENGENBARPHARANGES

4. Cut the cording into three equal lengths, knotting them together at one end.

5. Braid the cording as you rock and sway, braiding in your feathers and charms as you go. While you do this, hold an image in your mind of either the Witch Mother who is the Queen of Heaven and Hell, Mistress of the Crossroads, Lady of Elphame; or the Witch Father who is the Lord of Misrule, Auld Hornie, the Pukha. Feel free to chant, sing, or intone the barbarous words associated with the One whose protection you are invoking as you work.

6. When you come to the end of your cordage, tie an end knot to bind the rope.

7. Tie knots at or over each of your nine feathers or charms, starting in the middle and moving out, alternating sides. You may have to work carefully to keep from damaging the feathers as you pull them through the loops. Don't, however, take the shortcut of knotting as you work your way down the braid. That approach, while faster and easier, short circuits the power of the working because it disrupts the flow of energy into the braid as you work, and places the knots out of order.

8. When the knotting is completed, drape the rope and feathers around your neck and make an offering to the Witch Mother or Witch Father. (Use the Housle included in "Offerings," if you're unsure how to do this.)

Wear the rope and feathers each time you approach the Spirits of the Legion, especially when meeting or working with a Spirit who is unfamiliar to you. If you ever have need to unleash the power in your rope, you will need to make a new one.

Crafting a Dark Mirror

Materials Needed:
Glass surface (concave or flat)
Black enamel paint
Paint brush
Black fabric (felt, silk, velvet, wool)
Frame, stand, box (optional)
Adornments (optional)

Essentially, this tool is made by painting the backside of a piece of glass with black enamel (probably 2-3 coats to account for streaks). Enamel works best because it is both durable and glossy.

If you are using a concave piece of glass like a clock glass or an old-fashioned "bubbled" picture frame, you want to paint the outer bowl of the glass so that you will be looking into a clear, glossy black well or pool with the paint on the other side.

While the paint is still tacky, apply your black fabric to the entire backing. This will adhere to the enamel, adding an impenetrable layer of obscurity. No light will come through while you gaze into your mirror, and it will be protected from scratches.

You can encase the mirror in a frame or a wooden box (with a hinged lid, if you like), place it on a stand, or hang it on a wall.

Try to make the whole assembly of a size in which you'll be able to see your entire face at no further than arm's length away.

Embellish your dark mirror with runes, sigils, shells, stones, talismans, or other fetiches to enhance its power and lend you protection while you seek wisdom and guidance.

Creating the Lamps of Arte

Materials Needed:

2 Olive Oil Lamps (sealable canning jars with floating wicks)

Olive Oil

Herbs, as listed below

Your two Lamps will flank the Pyramid and represent the Sun and Moon. You can use any lamp or candle style that speaks to you, and many practitioners are referring to candles when they use the term "Lamps." You can adapt this method to make "dressed and fixed" candles, if you prefer. I like to use clear, pint-sized canning jars, olive oil, and floating wicks. The wicks are removed after each use, but the lamps can be sealed so the contents don't spill or become contaminated between uses.

As you layer your ingredients in the reservoir, start with rocks, then add minerals/metals, then dirts, roots, woods, resins, leaves, and finally flowers or berries. We're working from the ground up. Pour the olive oil last, almost filling the remainder of the reservoir.

Luna's Lamp

Smoky quartz

Silver charm or ring

Calamus root

Willow bark or twigs

Myrrh tears

Wormwood leaf

Jasmine blossoms

Assemble your Moon Lamp on the night of the New Moon. It should be dark outside while you work. Place all the ingredients, including the oil, in their proper order. Swirl the lamp three times every night at the same time until the next New Moon. Whisper this charm to your Moon Lamp as you work:

PHORBA PHORBOBAR BARO PHORPHOR PHORBAI

Sol's Lamp

Citrine	Cedarwood
Gold charm/ring	Dragon's Blood resin
OR Forge Dust	Mistletoe
Dandelion root	Calendula flowers

Assemble your Sun Lamp at sunrise of a Sunday. Swirl the lamp five times at sunrise each day consecutively for seven days. Intone this charm to your Sol Lamp as you work:

ABRAT ABRASAX SESENGENBARPHARANGES

Some part of each Lamp should be marked with the following symbols:

If your lamp has a glass hurricane shade, keep it free from soot and smudges.

In general, you may refill olive oil as needed without remaking the Lamps entirely. However, once per quarter, you should empty the reservoir and renew them by placing fresh ingredients and charming them as before. Only your silver and gold rings may be transferred from one lamp to the next.

Purification Incense

This blend is designed to help cleanse an object, person, or place — leaving them pure and ready for blessing (or whatever else comes next). This purification blend is slightly different in intention than the Banishing Incense recipe. While the Banishing blend is designed to clear an area of negativity, this Purification blend is designed with the intention to clean an area (or object or person) of anything "unclean" or unwanted.

As with all loose incense blends, this formula can be burned on a hot, self-igniting charcoal tablet (like those used for hookahs) or it can be thrown onto the glowing embers of a fire. You'll have to make it ahead of time, though, to give the components a chance to blend and dry out.

1/4 cup Lavender

1/4 cup Cedarwood

1/3 cup Rosemary

1/2 teaspoon Myrrh

1 teaspoon Copal

3 drops Frankincense oil

9 drops Florida Water

Spirit Conjuration (Invitation) Incense

This blend was designed to assist with the visionary, Spirit conjuration, and prophetic work of the Witch. It makes a relatively large batch, so you can scale it down, if needed.

1/2 cup Mugwort

1/4 cup Dittany of Crete

1/4 cup Lemongrass

1/4 cup Bay Laurel

1/4 cup Cedarwood chips

1/4 cup Heliotrope flowers

1/8 cup Myrtle leaves

2 tablespoons Frankincense tears

2 tablespoons Myrrh tears

3 drops Clary Sage essential oil

This incense is also wonderful for vision questing and flying out. It works in beautiful concert with flying ointment and Sabbat Wine/Tea.

Banishing Incense

This incense recipe is fantastic for clearing an area of negativity or for use in banishing spells. Use it to cleanse and clear an area before performing magick, as well — though it is STRONG for that purpose. (A bit like shouting: "EVERYBODY OUT!"

1/2 cup Cedarwood chips

1/2 cup Sage

1/4 cup Rowan Berries

1/4 cup Thyme

2 tablespoons Dragon's Blood resin

Pinch Cayenne

6 drops Wormwood oil

I sometimes like to add copal and myrrh to this recipe, as well, because I tend to prefer a very smoky banishing fume.

Khernips

Khernips is the sacred cleansing water of Ancient Greek ritual. It is sometimes called "lustral water," as it is used in lustration — the act of cleansing before entering the sanctuary. "Xernipstosai" (khernips-toe-sigh) means "to be purified." To enter the sacred space in an unclean state, according to Greek culture, can taint the people and objects inside and is also considered offensive to the Godds.

Flowing "living" water (rain, spring, river, ocean water, etc) is the simplest form of khernips, but it can also be created by combining the elements of Earth, Air, Fire, and Water.

Pour khernips over the hands of the ritual participants prior to entering the sacred space. You can also use it to sprinkle the entire space prior to ritual.

Mix a little salt (Earth) into a bowl of water. Light a stick of wood to create a Flame. I prefer palo santo, cedar, or white willow. Blow out the fire and allow the wood to smoke momentarily (Air). While smoking, plunge the glowing end into the saltwater.

Venus Water

Also known as Angel Water, Water of Venus originates in Europe — some say Portugal. Take note of Angel Water's scent when you use it, as the formula tends to smell different to each person who sniffs it. This is the aroma of the Morning and Evening Star made manifest for YOU.

Vodka base (I like Skyy for this, in its blue glass bottle)

Myrtle leaves

Orange oil

Rose hydrosol

Angelica root

This water is a wonderful aid in preparation and protection for Spirit work, and it can be quite successfully employed "In Case of Emergency" to usher an uncooperative or negative Spirit out of a space. When used in the latter capacity, sprinkle some Venus Water onto the scrying tool and over the Pyramid while speaking this arcane formula:

APO PANTOS KAKDAIMONOS

Ah-PAH PAHN-tohs kah-kah-DIE-moe-nohs

In Attic Greek, this means away from here, bad Spirits! *Kaka* as "bad" can be anything from uncooperative and mildly unpleasant to outright malicious.

Aligning the Three Souls

Grounding and centering are a common and thoroughly covered pair of practices among Witches and Mages. Taking some time to quiet one's inner chatter, put away day-to-day concerns, and connect to the ancient Powers is a necessary part of the Conjurer's Craft. Any effective practice that you've already developed to this end can be utilized.

The practice I use and teach is known as "Aligning the Three Souls." This or similar ritual can be found in the Feri Tradition, a Craft practice that differs from my own in some regards but which carries the very traditional and shamanic view of the tripartite Soul or the Triple Soul. Careful study shows us that shamans from many world cultures, including various expressions of European shamanism, share this concept, although the specifics can vary from culture to culture.

In my tradition, we talk about the Triple Soul in terms of the three sacred colors whose symbolism is so deeply woven into the Craft.

The White Soul

The White Soul is generally called the "Higher Self." In some traditions, it is called the "Holy Guardian Angel" (or HGA). Other names for this Soul from other religious systems include Augoeides (Neo-Platonism), Daemon (Platonism), Atman (Hinduism), Godd Self, etc.

Those who are able to see and interpret the aura often describe the White Soul as a crown or halo. In individuals with a very well-developed White Soul, this corona is often more visible and sometimes manifests as a visible star or bird above the head (especially when viewed in shamanic or highly receptive trance states).

Those on a path of enlightenment are said to be seeking "knowledge" of and "conversation" with the White Soul, and practices related to meditation, reflection, and invocation will all help the true seeker clarify their Soul's purpose and gain a better understanding of itself. Natural by-products of this "knowledge and conversation" are inspiration and wisdom.

The White Soul is the truest and purest Self, the Soul that is Godd-like in the sense that it is a Deity unto itself. It knows its Divinity and calls you to know it of yourself, as well. In rare glimpses throughout your mortal life, you will have true alignment of all Three Souls (as well as all Three Realms) and see yourself fully for the immortal and Divine Being you are.

The Red Soul

The Red Soul (or Bone Soul) is eternal and linked in a sort of alchemical marriage to the White Soul. Whereas the Black Soul is only with you for a single lifetime, your Red and White Souls are bound together throughout all your lives, deaths, and periods of rest and reflection that come in between.

We call the Red Soul the "Bone Soul" as a nod to both the blood-producing marrow that reminds us of our connection to the Witch Father and also because of this Soul's ability to connect us with those in our bloodline, both physically and spiritually. Here, we see the old maxim, "Blood calls to blood," play out again and again as we reincarnate into the same family lines in multiple lives or are connected to the same soul-mates in several incarnations. In this sense, the marrow is the Red Thread that connects the line of Witches back to Qayin. The Red Soul also acts as the thread that links the Black and White Souls, thereby connecting us to our Selves.

Where the Black Soul is responsible for our sense of self and identity in this life, and the White Soul is responsible for our sense of purpose and learning throughout all our lives, the Red Soul is the agent of our deepest connection to our world, our work, and our loved ones.

The Black Soul

The Black Soul is that part of the spirit that retains memories and the personality connected to a particular life. It is very individual, and it is separate from the Higher Self (White Soul) and the Eternal Soul (Red Soul). It is the part of the energy structure that may become a ghost, haunting a particular location; but more often, it is the Black Soul who acts as a guiding Ancestor for future generations.

If you've talked to the Mighty Dead via a medium, talking board, your own clairvoyance, or other tool, this is the Black Soul of that Ancestor. The White and Red Souls have remained together and gone on to do other work, probably as another incarnate being. The Black Soul has remained here to act as a guide.

While still living and working with the White and Red Souls as part of the YOU that you are right now, your Black Soul is able to leave your body through Witch flight and Fetch work. Some spiritual traditions call this astral travel. What they are calling the astral body, we are calling the Black Soul.

When Isobel Gowdie famously said, "I shall go into a hare," she was talking about sending her Black Soul out to roam in flight. The hare was a favorite choice of Fetch among Witches for its associations with the moon, shapeshifting, graveyards, and fertility.

To align these three Souls is synonymous with the more common parlance of grounding and centering. By engaging in this quick and simple practice, we bring our Souls into harmony and cooperation, still our minds, tap into the great Powers, and focus our Wills for whatever is to come.

I recommend performing this alignment daily as part of a morning routine, as well as prior to any ritual or sorcerous endeavors.

Three Soul Alignment

A helpful daily practice (and certainly one that is very effective for what many people would call "grounding and centering" prior to ritual) is that of bringing the Three Souls into alignment. This is simple and can be done with little fanfare, in a matter of a few short breaths. If your Sense of Arte favors more complicated ritual, there are certainly more elaborate accommodations that can be made.

Start by getting your feet planted or otherwise feeling your connection to the earth below you. Then state, "May the Three Souls be straight within me."

Continue by taking a deep breath out, sending your energy like a taproot into the earth. On the inhale, pull the earth's energy (and with it, the Forge Fire at the center of the earth) into your belly — the seat of the Black Soul (the Fetch, the personal identity, the Soul most connected with this life and your sense of Self).

On the next breath, pull the energy higher, to your chest — the seat of the Red Soul (the Bone Soul, the Ancestor connection through blood and fire).

On the third breath, pull the energy higher yet, to the skull, the crown of the head — the seat of White Soul (the higher self, the Holy Guardian Angel, the Godd-Self).

On the final breath, pull/push the energy all the way through yourself, connecting to the Star Fire above, releasing the breath with a sigh. You are connected to the Witch-Fire above and below, within and without. All three Soul-parts are connected and in harmony.

Cleansing, Shielding & Banishing

Cleansing the Space

Not every Witch cleanses and clears their working space prior to every ritual. That comes as a shock to Crafters who have been taught that such things absolutely must happen prior to all magick, sorcery, ritual, or conjuration. The difference between the two approaches boils down to philosophies around pollution and hallowing.

Miasma is the Greek term for a state of uncleanliness or pollution -- the absolute belief in which pervades many cultures, though the specifics vary greatly regarding which actions or events generate it. Most ancient and traditional cultures have an understanding that one should come before the Godds (or Powers) free from pollution. This includes both physical pollution as well as psychic or spiritual pollution. Bathing rituals are common across the world's religions because it is held as a sign of disrespect to approach Them in dirty clothes, smelling of body odor, and caked in grime from the day's toils. This concept is easy enough to understand, as many modern cultures would also view it as a sign of disrespect or carelessness, for instance, to greet professional colleagues by wiping the Chee-toh dust onto your sweatpants and saying, "Let's do this, bitches!" (as the popular Witchcraft meme goes).

In the same way that we can be physically "dirty" and therefore unprepared to approach Spirit, we can also be "dirty" on an Unseen level -- whether you consider it psychic, energetic, or spiritual will depend on the particulars of your cosmology and preferred Model(s) of Magick. More importantly, what you consider pollution-generating on the Unseen levels will be informed by the cultural traditions you've inherited and the magickal or sorcerous practice which you've adopted.

These cultural and magickal traditions will dictate your approach to cleansing both yourself and the space in which you perform your magickal work. It will also inform what you view as inherently sacred versus what needs to be consecrated (or hallowed) in order to become sacred. Many traditional practices, for instance, do not see the need to cleanse and consecrate a space dedicated to ritual and the Godds unless something has come in to disturb its otherwise enduring hallowed nature. In contemplating your own practice, you will want to consider whether or not your space serves multiple functions, is accessible to others, and whether it is outside or inside a building, as all of these can impact the frequency and intensity with which you cleanse it.

I'll share my own philosophies and practices as a point of reference. If you don't already have your own in place, they can serve as a starting point in helping you determine what you consider sacred and profane -- and pure versus polluted. If you already have practices in place, comparing and contrasting with mine might give you greater insight into what you've been doing and why.

When I am able to work in a space dedicated to the Arts, I do not cleanse it prior to every rite. I will, however, use the "Cleansing Chants" that follow to do quarterly maintenance, as well as any "as needed" cleansing if something comes up. This could include a spiritual or physical intrusion, deep or unpleasant Shadow Work that feels like it's hanging around, etc. I'll also cleanse before and after having guests in the space -- anyone who isn't cord-bound in my Tradition and regularly sharing the ritual space with me. I think of it as something akin to putting fresh sheets on a bed for a guest -- and changing them again after they leave.)

If I'm working in space that isn't dedicated to Craft -- and especially if I'm working in a space that sees a lot of traffic or the ups-and-downs of daily living -- I prefer to use the "Cleansing Chants" prior to every ritual. This has been my habit (and a result of my training) when doing rites in living rooms, backyard that see a lot of family life, public beaches/parks, and retreat cabins/lodges. These spaces accumulate the "yuck" of our physical and emotional pain, and the hallowing wears thin due to mundane usage.

For the "big" rites (namely initiations, but also certain workings that are far-reaching and weighty), I will perform the Star Ruby ritual or the Craft version of the Lesser [Banishing] Ritual of the Pentagram. They are very similar to each other in construction and result, however, the Star Ruby is performed entirely in Attic Greek, while the standard LBRP is performed in the operator's native language with a few phrases and names coming from Hebrew traditions. In my Craft Tradition, we've created a Witch's LBRP (shared below), which includes four Latin words but is otherwise spoken in one's native language. It's worth noting that these particular cleansing and centering rites are a daily practice for many Mages, as well as being a practice for preparing the ritual grounds. The Witch's LBRP was humbly offered to the blogosphere by me and my Sisters for Crafters who are drawn to such a practice. (It is oriented to the Quarters and Castles/Watchtowers of our Trad, so feel free to adapt it for your use, as needed.)

Regarding the cleansing of my person, I come physically clean to every ritual, but I don't necessarily bathe immediately prior to each rite. If I bathed (in a mundane sense) at some point earlier in the day and didn't sweat, have sex, or do dirty work (housecleaning, gardening, etc) then I feel sufficiently clean for most types of rites. (I liken this to showering in the morning, doing office work through the day, and then having a dinner date in the evening. In *most* cases, I won't feel like I need to shower again before dinner.)

Prior to all ritual, I will employ khernips — or the combination of another blessed water along with incense smoke. I use these by applying them to my hands, face, and heart, for a simple cleansing. When I feel moved by intuition to do so, I will also apply the khernips (or water and smoke) to my belly and feet. Doing so, of course, addresses all three seats of the Soul and is a reminder of the Fivefold Kiss.

Some rituals, though, require more preparation. Initiations, weddings, funerals, and other rites of passage really deserve a special bath or shower. In these cases, I take a shower to clean my body, followed by a ritual bath replete with dressed candle and bath sachet (shared at the end of this chapter). This provides a cleansing by Water and Fire — a powerful combo.

Shielding

An energetic or psychic shield is in place for most people most of the time. Folks who engage in energy work should recognize the sensation of lowering this most basic built-in energy shield in order to let another person connect with us in some intimate, personal way. Phrases like "having one's walls up" and "being guarded" are acknowledgments of this most basic and somewhat unconscious method of shielding.

As a Witch and certainly as a Conjurer you'll want and need a variety of shields for different occasions. You'll also want to be able to lower them in full or in part and change them in other ways, as needed. I suggest meeting new Spirits with a moderate shield in place. You may choose to lower or thin it if needed for communication or other connections, or raise / thicken it further for protection.

Try some exercises to practice manipulating your shields before you begin conjuring Spirits. For instance you could build elemental shields; experiment with gemstone shields if you are sensitive to stones' energies; play with light, texture, and color to see how this changes your experience; try using different materials such as steel, and array of woods, and different types of cloth fabric, etc.

Playing and experimenting with your shields will help you better understand what might work best as you approach new Spirits. Don't be shy about when and where you try these on for size. After all, we're all using some type of shield as we interact with the world. You may even find that sensitive individuals make comments about how they perceive you differently with different shields in place.

To create an energetic shield, you will start by grounding and centering ("Aligning the Three Souls"). You don't want to create your shield from your personal energy stores, per se. While that could be fine for your basic needs most of the time, it can also be very draining. In fact, if you are a Highly Sensitive Person (HSP -- as described by Elaine Aron), as I find that a good number of Witches are, you may find yourself very often drained by everyday interactions with others. Learning how to manage your boundaries, interpersonal as well as energetic, will go a very long way in helping to give you balance and peace so you can accomplish those things that you have set as priorities without losing your mind.

So, yes, ground and center and gather energy from Above and Below. You are always at the center of your own Compass, whether you are intentionally laying a Compass or not. So you can draw on the energies around you at any time if you are grounded and centered.

If you have done some basic energy ball exercises in the past, you likely focused on bringing energy to your palms. (If you haven't done this before, you can try now.) For shielding, you bring the energy outward through your whole body.

Your energetic body naturally extends for several inches past your physical body. Some people are able to see this energetic body. There are cameras that can photograph it. Certain cultures have names for the different layers of the energetic/spiritual body (bodies).

When we create an energetic shield, we are often extending that energetic body a little further and always reinforcing its outer perimeter. In its natural state, it allows other energy to flow through it -- ours goes out, others' comes in. The more empathic you are, the more you pick up on other people's emotions, moods, and physical illnesses, etc through this sort of energy exchange. You can also be extremely sensitive to physical energies like those from gemstones or woods or other objects with their own inherent power or life force.

By way of example:

I was at a psychic fair a few years ago and had just purchased a moldavite ring. Fantastic stone! I bought it because I consider it a powerful representation of Witch Fire -- specifically of Tubelo's Green Fire (the cunning fire, the green fire between the eyes of the Dragon at the Fall of the Angels). It's a star-stone (tektite). Specifically, it's a type of glass created when a meteorite struck a particular area in what is now the Czech Republic. I had to build up a sort of tolerance to this stone when I first came into contact with it. I could look, but I couldn't touch it for long. It made the top of my head tingle and vibrate so forcefully that it could trigger a migraine for me. So the day I bought it, I put it in my pocket at the store where I was working as a Tarot reader and returned to the psychic fair around the corner where I later joined a conversation with a group of people I had just met. About five minutes into the chat, a young man started to swoon, and said, "I'm sorry, I don't know what's wrong. I was doing fine, but I feel really dizzy all of a sudden." We got him in a chair and asked the usual questions about whether he was hydrated and fed. I stepped away for a moment and when I came back, he rather shockingly said it was me that made him dizzy. He was fine when I left, and tilt-a-whirl when I returned. It was only then that I remembered the moldavite and the reaction I normally had to it. I was starting to build my tolerance to it, but this guy was even more sensitive than me.

To test me theory, I took it out of my pocket and sent it away with a friend (not showing or telling him what it was). He was immediately fine. He later came over to my booth to have a look at the ring and almost passed out when I unwrapped it from the bag! Needless to say, that young man was not likely to ever buy moldavite for himself. It was practically kryptonite, in his case. I, on the other hand, wear my ring every time I do ritual work (and often just when I want a boost).

The point of the story is that as Witches, we need to be aware that we need good shields in our daily lives for more than just "negative energies." Social media these days is very fond of reminding us to sage our homes and put quartz in our windows and "clear the negativity away." I'd rather Witches remember that we need balance. We need to take care of ourselves, and sometimes that means understanding that what is absolutely fabulous for someone else can make us sick or weak or off-kilter. It is our responsibility to know where our boundaries are and to reinforce them. Our shields are one of the ways we can do that.

Two Basic Types of Shields

You might think it's a little simplistic to say that shields come in two basic flavors, and you're right. We're going to talk in a minute about how you can make them as complex and unique as your specific energy signature. But in terms of basic function, your shields are going to do one of two things (more or less). They will either be:

Receptive, or

Reflective

Like it says on the tin, a receptive shield (essentially) takes in the energy, and a reflective shield sends it back.

Now, HOW they do that is where all the cool, fun, and creative bits happen. This is where your imagination and force of Will come into play.

Shield Construction & Composition

Your intention for the shield and how you visualize the energy forming around you determine what the shield looks, feels, and functions like.

You can decide if you want the shield to be permeable in one or both directions so you can send and/or receive energy (to/from loved ones, perhaps; or even sensations from co-workers or others with whom you would normally maintain some sort of link).

You can also decide how thick, tough/hard, etc the outer walls of the shield will be. Some shields might work best for you if they are thick and gelatinous like placenta or a hard-boiled egg-white. Others might need to be 10-foot thick concrete walls. Some might only need to be a thin bubble-layer membrane.

Shields can be composed of raw (and also specific) elemental energy as well as the energy of specific stones, trees, animals, and natural forces. As you practice and work with this type of magick, you can create thunderstorm shields, oak leaf shields, raven shields, amethyst shields, etc.

Finally, you can layer multiple shields, so that you have inner and outer walls of protection. Maybe you always keep your innermost shield up, have a mid-range shield that you lower at home with your partner or closest friends (unless they're on edge), and have an outer shield that is in place any time you leave your home or have company over.

Infinite Applications

So, even though I said above that there are two basic types of shields (receptive and reflective), you can see that there are really an infinite number of specific shields available to the inventive Witch. Let's take a look at a few examples, just for kicks and giggles.

- Receptive thick stone wall shield like the "castillo" forts intended to catch and hold incoming energy, where it will be neutralized & absorbed
- Receptive lava flow shield intended to melt incoming negativity (erected only during suspected/known confrontation)
- Receptive cotton batting shield intended to filter and cushion off-hand negativity and harshness (as an inner shield)
- Reflective clear quartz mirror shield with high shine and faceted cuts intended to send amplified energy back to originating source
- Reflective hurricane shield intended to send negative energy back to its source along with powerful destruction

I think you get the picture. The possibilities are endless. My advice, if this is new for you, is to start simple with something you can visualize and maintain for an extended period of time. You can build on the skill from there.

Releasing (& Cutting Off) Energy

We've talked a lot about getting the energy flow started and rolling, but there may be times where you need to detach from it. There are a couple of ways you can do this. The simplest is using visualization.

There is an effective tree visualization for grounding and centering, which involves sending your energy roots and limbs out. Using the same visualization in reverse should be an effective way to disengage from an overstimulating energetic experience, if needed. Simply draw your "roots and limbs" back in toward yourself and strengthen your shields. (Actually, I'll add here that some people find disconnecting from the energy but connecting to the physical earth is very helpful to diffuse the excess energy in their systems.)

Another method that can be helpful is running your hands under cold tap water for a few moments. Similarly, saltwater is very helpful, as is Florida Water. To use these, you can either dip your hands and feet into a small amount or sprinkle them onto your hands, feet, crown of the head, chest, and back of the heart. (These are the energy centers I find most effective. You may find that you need to focus somewhere other than the heart and head. The belly, perhaps. Maybe only the hands.)

You might also consider keeping a large stone that you pour excess energy into, like a battery that you can draw from at a later time when you are feeling low. Quartz is always a good choice for this, but there may be another that would work equally well for you.

Banishing

Do not call upon any unfamiliar Spirit unless and until you also know how to send them away if the need arises. Nine times out of 10, Spirits whose demeanors range from helpful and friendly to aloof and neutral will leave on their own when the work for which you called them is done. Occasionally they will want to hang around to continue checking you or the situation out. Very infrequently, one of these neutral to good Spirits will need to have their invitation rescinded and be sent away. From my own experience and observation, I find that Spirits who need to be told to leave and leave now are either uninvited in the first place, or they are on the neutral to negative side of the alignment. They'll either say something that raises the hackles, or their presence is somehow uncomfortable.

Remember, there are several Spirits who didn't merit being put on the "Do Not Call" list, but who are difficult or problematic in their own way. If you choose to call on one of these, go into the conjuration with your shields up and the secure knowledge that you can dismiss them if they become bothersome.

A moment ago, I mentioned Spirits sometimes showing up uninvited. Don't be overly alarmed by this idea. For one thing, it does not happen very frequently. When and if it does, it is important to remember that this is not so different from getting unsolicited messages on social media, in some respects. You've made yourself available for contact, and sometimes you're contacted by folks you don't know. That contact can be anything from "Hey, I saw that thing you did and I dig it. Let's be friends!" to "Check out this picture of my genitals that you absolutely didn't request and probably don't enjoy." More often than not, it's more like spam. annoying, unnecessary, and not a direct threat unless you engage.

Banishing is an act that sends an unwelcome Spirit away from your space. Some practitioners banish as a means of saying goodbye to any Spirit. Personally I prefer "farewell" over "f*** off" in most cases, and banishing feels a lot more like the latter.

There are lots of ways to banish, when/if that need arises. You can:

- *Ring a bell*. The sound vibrations from metal bells have been used for centuries to send negative Spirits away. Iron and brass bells are viewed as more effective for this purpose than other types of metals. They both have long traditions in Spirit work, with a good deal of lore ascribed to each of them.

- *Speak a charm or formula*. Traditional favorites are **Hekas, o hekas, este bebeloi** and **Apo pantos kakadaimonos**. You could also perform an entire Witches' LBRP. Shouting or saying firmly "Get out" also works quite nicely. Remember that not all Words of Power come to us from classical or barbarous languages.

- <u>*Light a candle*</u> that has been dressed for this purpose.
- <u>*Asperge the area with a blessed water*</u> like khernips, Florida Water, or Venus Water.
- <u>*Sprinkle salt*</u>. This mineral has been used for millennia as a ward against unwelcome entities.
- <u>*Smoke the area with a cleansing incense*</u> like one of those shared in this book.

Any of these can be done individually to send a Spirit away. I tend to start with "Get out" and go from there. Pairing any two of these is effective enough for me that I've generally not needed to resort to the "In Case Of Emergency" suggestions later in this book. However if you've tried what you can from this list and are still being vexed, then check there for the nuclear options.

Ritual Bath (with Candle & Sachet)

There are two things you want to happen as part of this cleansing. You want the light of the dressed candle to touch you while it burns. This is a fire cleansing. And you want to immerse yourself in the bath water three times.

If you don't have a tub, don't fit in the tub, or have mobility issues that would make this impossible or dangerous for you, get creative. Fill a bucket that you soak the sachet in, and pour this over yourself three whole times. Soak that sachet in the water each time, and get every bit of you wet. (Do this in your shower, obviously.) Or, if even this is genuinely not possible, pour the sachet-infused water over your head three times and use it to wash your hands and heart three times each.

Dressed Candle

Dress a white chime candle using a small amount of your anointing oil (VanVan or simple vervain oil both work great) and purification incense. This is the candle you will burn during your preparatory bath.

Bath Sachet

Place the following 13 herbs in a muslin drawstring bag or cotton/linen hankie tied with a string (or prepare as an infusion and add the strained liquid to your bath water):

Angelica root	Peppermint
Arnica flowers	Rosemary
Bay leaves	Rue
Eucalyptus	Sage
Hyssop	Thyme
Lemongrass	Vervain
Lavender	

Cleansing Chants

Each portion of the chant requires a Witch to walk the Compass either once or thrice, wielding the appropriate (and obvious) cleansing tools.

> Smoke and fume, now as you burn,
> cause all harm from us to turn;
> let nothing harmful here be found,
> as we tread the Witch's round.

> Fire that burns and light that glows,
> send all harm away from us;
> let nothing harmful here be found,
> as we tread the Witch's round.

> Water and salt, brine of the sea,
> wash this circle clean and free;
> let nothing harmful here be found,
> as we tread the Witch's round.

> Besom sweep and besom clean;
> above, below and in between;
> let nothing harmful here be found,
> as we tread the Witch's round.

Witch's LBRP

No tools are required for this ritual.

The Qabbalistic Cross

Imagine a ball of light above your head. Reach up with your right hand and grab the light. When you touch yourself with that hand, part of the light will go into you.

Touch your forehead as you say "**Corona**" (Crown). Let it fill with the light.

Touch your pelvis at the pubic bone and say "**Serpens**" (Serpent). Let it fill with light.

Touch your right shoulder and say "**Clementia**" (Mercy). Let it fill with light.

Touch your left shoulder and say "**Severitas**" (Severity). Let it fill with light.

Hold your hands in prayer over your heart and say "**Benedictiones**" (Blessings). Let it fill with light.

Feel your whole body fill with the cross of light.

The Pentagrams

Face East. Before you in the air, draw a giant pentagram using your right index finger (or if you prefer use the whole hand). Imagine that pentagram shining in front of you. Take a step forward with your left foot. Just the left. Leave your right one where it is. The size of the step will be determined by your space. At the same time that you step forward, thrust your open hands, side by side, palms downward, into the pentagram, as if you are diving in. This is called the "Sign of the Enterer." As you enter the pentagram you will say one of the names of the Witch God or Goddess.

Here, at the first pentagram you will *shout* "**Lucifer**." Lucifer is the Light-Bringer, the Lord of Illumination of the World and the Mind. He is called in the East as the bright aspect of Tubal Cain, and the lord of elemental Fire. Lucifer is called with a jubilant shout to celebrate the rising of the sun in the East.

Step back with your left foot so it is once again beside your right foot. Touch your right index finger to your lips like you are making the "Shhh, no talking" gesture. Point your right index finger to the center of the pentagram and make a quarter turn to your right. As you do so, draw an imaginary arc of white light around to the next direction.

Draw a pentagram in the South. Enter the pentagram while *singing* "**Goda**." Goda is the White Goddess, the Queen of the Seelie Court and Lady of Death-in-Life. She rules the Southern quadrant, the place of elemental Earth. Her name is sung for she is the Lady who shall "have music wherever She goes."

Make the "shhh" gesture and turn to the right, drawing an arc.

Draw a pentagram in the West. Enter the pentagram *intoning* "**Azazel**" in a low voice. Azazel is the Lord of the West, the place of elemental Water. He is Tubal Cain in his aspect as the Lord of the Dead, and is both the angel who taught magick to the daughters of man and the angel who collects our Souls for their great rest. The West is the place where the sun goes to die, and it is to the West that we all must travel upon death. Azazel's name is intoned in a low voice of mourning and respect.

Make the "shhh" gesture and turn to the right, drawing an arc.

Draw a pentagram in the North. Enter the pentagram *whispering* "**Kolyo**." Kolyo is the Black Goddess, the Weaver of Fate and the Lady of Life-in-Death. She rules the North, which is the home of elemental Air. Her name is whispered for she is an ancient mystery.

Make the "shhh" gesture and turn to the right, drawing an arc. This final arc connects all four pentagrams into a single circle.

The Watchtowers

You are now standing in the center of a circle of white light. At each quarter there is a giant, glowing pentagram. Now we post a Watchtower between each pentagram. Face the southeast and open up your arms. Stretch out like you are a cross: feet together, arms out at shoulder height. Call the Watchtowers to their posts. Stand in the cross position and say:

"Before me stands the Castle of Stone. Behind me stands the Castle of Glass. On my right stands the Castle Perilous. On my left stands the Castle of Revelry."

These are four of the great castles of myth and legend. The Castle of Stone is Caer Bannog, the Castle of Glass is Glastonbury, the Castle Perilous is the silvery Grail Castle, and the Castle of Revelry is the Golden

Castle of the Beacon of Awen.

Spread your feet and lift your arms to stand in pentagram-position and say: "Around me flame the pentagrams. Above me shines a six-rayed star, and below me spins a three-armed triskle. I stand within the Spiral Castle. I am the World Tree." This declaration places you in all three realms, and allows you to traverse shamanic space. It states that you are the World Tree, and that you ride the Stang to other realms.

The Qabbalistic Cross (Closing)

Now repeat the Qabbalistic Cross as you began.

Imagine a ball of light above your head. Reach up with your right hand and grab the light. When you touch yourself with that hand, part of the light will go into you.

Touch your forehead as you say "**Corona**" (Crown). Let it fill with the light.

Touch your pelvis at the pubic bone and say "**Serpens**" (Serpent). Let it fill with light.

Touch your right shoulder and say "**Clementia**" (Mercy). Let it fill with light.

Touch your left shoulder and say "**Severitas**" (Severity). Let it fill with light.

Hold your hands in prayer over your heart and say "**Benedictiones**" (Blessings). Let it fill with light.

Feel your whole body fill with the cross of light.

Laying the Compass & Building the Pyramid

My way is not the only way. I hope to be clear on that point, as I feel too many writerly Witches provide methods in their books and act as though they are holy writ -- unyielding and unalterable by mortal folk. That's just not so. You're free to use this Compass and Pyramid method exactly as written, adapt it to a method that works better for you, or use a different approach entirely.

First, a note on this method. When Witches of my Tradition lay a Compass, we are creating an energetic crossroads within what is sometimes called a "moat." This moat is a boundary that demarcates our Millgrounds -- the area within which we work. The crossroads are formed by opening the gates at the cardinal directions in opposing pairs. North/Air and South/Earth. East/Fire and West/Water.

Ceremonial Magick (and Wicca, as a result of CM's early influences) doesn't create this crossroads within its circle casting. The energies aren't called in a pair of opposites that face each other. Instead the elements are positioned such that energy works on something like an electromagnetic principle and is pushed from one quarter to the next around the circle. This is a very workable approach which should be obvious based on its popularity. It's just not typically one I employ.

The system I'm sharing with you is one that puts you at the center of the crossroads — a powerful place of sorcery. You access the World Tree there, and you're able to travel upon it to any world. You are the balance point between all the elements. Between day and night. Between life and death.

Most Ceremonial Mages place the Pyramid (which they call the Triangle of Arte) in the East (Air, for them) when they do Goetic workings. They have their own symbolism and rationale for orienting the Pyramid this way. However I would suggest that the Pyramid either be placed in the quadrant from which you call Earth (South in the system I share here) or in the direction the Spirit is associated with, if applicable. Placing the Pyramid in one of these positions allows for easier manifestation by the Spirit.

Closing the Ritual

A great many Craft Traditions and practices have a specific method for "closing the circle" or ending the ritual. Since we think of the Compass as being ever present, and our actions to lay it as being a way to draw the attention of the Powers, the Witches of my Tradition don't "unmake" the space at the end of the working. Rather, for us, the Red Meal (or Housle) is the natural conclusion of the rite. Some of us add a "So Mote It Be" or a "Thus the work is complete" at the very end to give a sense of closure. I like clapping three times following such a declaration.

If you desire to unmake the Compass after you've bid the Spirit farewell, I recommend the following:

Address each of the Gates in the opposite order they were called, moving counterclockwise if you called in a generally clockwise direction, or vice versa. Say something like "Gatekeeper of the North, this rite is at an end. With my thanks, I ask you to close the way. So Mote It Be!"

Laying the Compass

The Compass is laid by setting the caim — defining the area of protection and power within which the Witch or Coven will perform the work. For this method, we call Powers that lie opposite each other as a pair — both being called toward the center of the circle. Thus, they form a road or an energetic pathway, with the Stang as the center point.

I prefer to begin with all the tools and materials either on my person (like cords and knives), or placed in a basket at the Center of the Compass. From there, I move things into place, as appropriate. You may also place the items in their final locations before beginning. If your ritual is very simple, or if you work with a minimum of tools, you may choose to keep everything at the base of the Stang and not place anything at the Gates. The choice is entirely yours.

Raise the Stang

Stand with the Stang in the center of your Compass space. (If you have a full complement of tools, you might secure it in a holder, if you have one, using a personal Stang or Distaff to Lay the Compass. If not, feel free to use this one Stang as needed, placing it upright in its central holder wherever it isn't needed as a working tool in your hands.) The cauldron is placed behind the Stang, and the anvil (or Oath Stone) is placed in front of it, with the hammer on top. If you don't have these tools yet, make do. A forked stick, a bowl, and a stone will serve, if needed. Take a moment to energetically connect with the energy of the Forge-fire at the center of the Earth, far below the iron foot of the Stang; and also connect with Star-fire in the heavens, high above but still between the horns of the Stang. Breathe deeply and say, "May the three souls be straight within me." Feel yourself centered.

Marking the Moat

Using your Stang, walk the perimeter of the space, moving in a circle. Mark a circle on the ground by either dragging the Stang or dragging one of your feet. Allow this "uneven step" to remind you that you walk between worlds. The Seen and the Unseen are ever present. The Living and the Dead are both here. As one of the Cunning Folk, you lay this Compass as a reminder that the hedge is this, and you straddle it.

You may chant the following Compass Charm as you walk: "ZETA TSEDA ZYIDA SZYADA"

Open the Gates

The first gate you open should be the one in which you are working. This example begins in the South, as I have recommended that as a great general place for Spirit manifestation. If the Spirit is said to arrive from a particular direction, start with that gate instead.

Stand in the Center and face the South. Hold both

arms down by your sides, palms flat and facing the ground. Say, "I call to the Fields beyond the South Gate. Open the door from the South, place of Earth, Goda's domain. By the plate, the soil, and the shield, I call you to open wide the Gate and send forth your road to the center of this, my Compass. So mote it be!"

Turn to the North. Hold both arms up, fingers spread wide. Say, "I call to the Winds beyond the North Gate. Open the door from the North, place of Air, Kolyo's domain. By the spear, the wing, and the smoke, I call you to open wide the Gate and send forth your road to the center of this, my Compass. So mote it be!"

Turn to the West. Hold your arms out in front of you, hands cupped. Say, "I call to the Ocean beyond the West Gate. Open the door from the West, place of Water, Azazel-Qayin's domain. By the cup, the quench tank, and the helm, I call you to open wide the Gate and send forth your road to the center of this, my Compass. So mote it be!"

Turn to the East. Hold one arm up, fist raised. Say, "I call to the Sunrise beyond the East Gate. Open the door from the East, place of Fire, Lucifer-Qayin's domain. By the steel, the anvil, and the sun, I call you to open wide the Gate and send forth your road to the center of this, my Compass. So mote it be!"

Thus is the Compass laid. Proceed, now, to Building the Pyramid.

Building the Pyramid

Materials:

Wooden/cloth triangle OR sticks/stones
Soil from the Millgrounds
Invitation Incense
2 Lamps of Arte (Luna and Sol)

The Pyramid is built after the Compass has been laid. Place the boundary marking for your Pyramid (or Triangle of Arte) outside the Moat in the direction from which you expect the Spirit to arrive. (Place it in the South, if not specified.) Place Luna's Lamp to the left and Sol's Lamp to the right of the Pyramid.

Your Pyramid may be a painted wooden form, an embroidered cloth, an outline fashioned by laying three equal-length

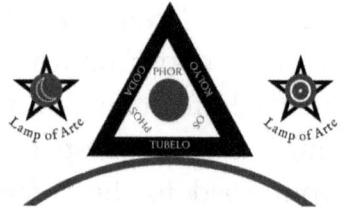

sticks end-to-end, or of any material your choose. It may be elaborate or simple, as pleases you.

Sprinkle each side of your Pyramid with either soil from the land upon which you are working or a portion of the Invitation Incense, speaking aloud the three names you ascribe to the three sides of the Tringle, with the following request:

"Goda, give the Spirit form.
Kolyo, give the Spirit voice.
Tubelo, give the Spirit time here with me.
Iarbatha! So be it!"

Light the two Lamps of Arte that flank the Pyramid and prepare for the Invitation.

Invitation & Farewell

After your Compass is laid and your Pyramid constructed, you are ready to summon the Spirit you've chosen to contact.

Actually, I'm a little leery of the term and intention behind the word "summon" in this context -- as well as its partner, "dismiss." I don't want to belabor the semantics of the thing too much, but both "summon" and "dismiss" have a connotation of commanding and compelling, as if the Spirit is powerless to object or follow their own will in the matter. Indeed phrases like "summon stir and call ye forth" are used side by side with "I command and compel you." I don't know about you, but I'm never *summoned* by anyone who sees me as an equal. Summoning seems to be reserved for those in the highest of power — like judges. Even most employers understand that they need to speak and deal with workers from a clear place of basic respect. Whether the relationship we are building is filial, romantic, or business like, you should start it the way you plan for it to continue. Respectfully, cooperatively, reciprocally.

This means inviting the Spirit to join you as you might invite a friend to join you for dinner or a work colleague for a meeting. Much like those examples, this meeting will involve communication and should offer both you and the Spirit some benefit. It's an opportunity to explore a partnership, at its core. That partnership may last only as long as the ritual, or it may continue throughout your lifetime.

If you've never communicated with a Spirit before, you won't always know their personality or preferences well enough to make a customized invitation. The one provided here should be good for calling on any Spirit (aside from the eight "Do Not Calls"). Adapt it if you like, or devise your own, as you get to know Spirits well.

All the same principles apply for the Spirit's departure at the end of the ritual. Instead of dismissing them (which comes across as callous and superior) or banishing them (which is unnecessarily aggressive and antagonistic if the interaction was otherwise positive), I suggest bidding the Spirit a cordial farewell. In fact, if/when you've developed a close relationship with a Spirit, you might even incorporate the phrase "Stay if you will; go if you must", which acknowledges the Spirit's agency in the matter and also reiterates that you enjoy their presence even when there is no immediate business at hand.

Your farewell should come after the Housle, your sacrificial meal.

Invitation

Sprinkle incense on glowing charcoal in your incense dish.

Say: "By the setting Sun and rising Moon, by the falling Star and the fixed Star, I call unto [Spirit name]! Come quickly, by your power, and appear to me here on Earth. Hither to me, mighty Spirit, I call you. Potent, boundless, indescribable [Spirit name]: Be present with me this night that we might make compact (or communicate). This sweet smoke I offer, and cakes and red wine. Be firmly here, and be welcome."

End by saying this formula:

IAEÕBAPHRENEMOUN IARBATHA

(ee-ah-oh bah-PRAY-nay-moon ee-ar-BAH-ta)

Farewell

After the Housle, say: "Go, blessed Spirit, as you will to that place where you live eternally. Go with my thanks."

Say:

IARBATHA! So be it!

Methods & Techniques of Spirit Communication

In our "order of service," we have now come to the part labeled "Knowledge and Conversation." Ultimately, talking or otherwise engaging with the Spirit is why you have enacted your ritual. Whether or not you make a Compact, give the Spirit a vessel, or even reach out to them again is likely to be determined by the conversation you have. That conversation can take many shapes and could involve one of several dozen communication tools. If you are able and choose to engage in conversation with a Spirit without the use of tools, you are engaging in clairvoyance, clairaudience, or clairsentience, depending on the manner in which you perceive the Spirit's message. We will discuss how to use a few of the tools, which will ultimately strengthen your ability with the "clairs."

Before we dig into a few of them, I'd like to give you this word of advice: Don't be discouraged if you initially struggle to communicate with a Spirit. These are skills which require training and practice. If you've never communicated with any Spirit before, you are likely to doubt yourself a bit. This is normal. You might try using the same techniques to communicate with one or more of your Ancestors before beginning Goetic work. The Dead with whom we have family bonds by blood or adoptive oath are quick to come to us and often a little easier to perceive than other Spirits. Build your skill and confidence with an Ancestor who is open to helping you, and then come back to a Goetic practice feeling more prepared.

With every sense by which you can perceive, a Spirit can communicate. Some make themselves seen and show us a series of mental images to convey their messages. Some make themselves heard, speaking to our minds directly or through a text-based medium like a talking board or automatic writing. Some will convey knowledge through tactile sensation, making us feel what they have to share. A few even use taste and smell to convey or enhance their messages. With some, a sense of inexplicable knowing comes to you, as if the information popped into your head from nowhere. A great many Spirits use a combination of these senses all in the same session. (Astaroth comes to mind as a Spirit who is verbal and visual and also has a strong olfactory presence.)

Likewise, you probably have a preferred way or combination of ways that you receive messages best. You may already have a solid metacognitive awareness regarding how you think and perceive the world. Maybe you already know that you are a very verbal person, for example — one who paints the world with their words and remembers phrases and whole sentences long after they were spoken. Or maybe you haven't had reason to develop this insight about yourself yet. That's great, too! You'll get to experiment and discover a new skill set.

Some of the methods we'll discuss can blend together and be used in combination. There's no rule written that says you can't hear while you scry, or that you can't get clairvoyant / visual messages while you use a talking board. I find that Spirits use whatever combination of their strengths that mesh with our own. Bear that in mind as I share techniques and thoughts related to these few methods. I may be writing about them separately, but you don't have to use them that way.

Seething

To "seethe" means to "boil." It is a way to set your own essence, your own Spirit, to boil — to roll and move within you. At its core, seething is achieved by sinking into any trance-inducing movement. You can be seated, swaying and rocking and circling your torso and your head. You can be standing, allowing your hips, legs, and feet to sway or circle, too. or you can be fully ambulatory, dancing, twirling, running, and moving throughout your Millgrounds as your Spirit is moved.

The purpose of seething is twofold. It can be a means to raise energy toward a purpose. In our case, that purpose would be Spirit manifestation and communication. Or seething can induce a "visionary" state in which messages are received or Spirit journeying is performed. I say "visionary" (with quotes) because the messages might be visual or they might be aural or tactile, etc.

Seething in Witchcraft is a direct descendant of "*seidhr*"-ing in Norse Magic. The trance of the *seidhkona* or *seidhman* is essentially the same as our own seething practice. As such there are a few pointers we might take to enhance the experience.

One is the use of the staff — or Stang. Our Stang, too, is a direct descendant (on its mother's side) from the völva's *stav*, which was either a wooden staff or an iron tool resembling a weaver's distaff. The stav was an extension of Yggdrasil. It was a personal, portable World Tree. It becomes the hobby horse on which we ride into other worlds. Our own Sleippnir — eight legged like the spokes on the Year Wheel. One leg for each world that we might access from Midgard, this middle realm.

Try seething with your Stang or staff. Tap a rhythm with it on the ground, or tap the rings on your hand to the pole. Chant. Try chanting or intoning the names of the Spirit. Lose yourself in the rhythm and rush and movement, and know that your riding pole will center you to this world while you seek wisdom that comes from others.

Another thing we know from both ancient accounts and modern practitioners is that the *seidhkona* or *seidhman* "fell" into a trance. That is, at a climactic point in their movement, they would fall to the ground spent, and this is when the visions would come the clearest. I suspect that breath work and alteration of blood flow, both of which would come naturally as part of the exertion just described, are at least partially responsible for the trance state and visions.

Finally, this type of trance was often accompanied by entheogens — journey drugs that were either carried in a pouch on the body of the *seidhkona* or *seidhman* or ingested in some way. Both cannabis and henbane seeds have been found at the burial sites of several *völur* (staff-carrying magick-working women who were praised as seers). As Witches, we might employ a "flying ointment" or drink a "Sabbat wine" infused with vision-aiding herbs. My favorite is a very sweet dessert red wine in which I've steeped mugwort and lemon balm, with lots of local honey to dial back the bitterness of the mugwort.

Scrying

Whether you use a mirror, crystal/stone sphere, cauldron of water, incense smoke, melted candle wax, or a hearth/campfire, the process of scrying progresses along the same general path. The main differences come in two ways. First, the elemental influence of the chosen scrying tool will play a part in the work. And second, the reflectiveness or lack thereof inherent in the tool will also impact the ease and accessibility for some. Conventional wisdom holds that it is easier to learn to scry in a reflective surface like a mirror, quartz ball, or bowl of water. I prefer to choose my scrying medium based on the nature of the Spirit with whom I'm working.

The basic process is this: You will enter a meditative state, relax your gaze while looking in the direction of your scrying tool or element, and then simply allow the messages or images to come to you. If you are using a cauldron, water goblet, quartz ball, or dark mirror, it is helpful to do this work in a darkened room with only your Lamps of Arte for illumination. Their light should be diffusely illuminating the room (casting a glow onto the surface of the water or glass), but not directly in your line of vision. (Actually, limiting other visual stimuli while scrying is often helpful, though the more you practice this technique, the more you will develop your own tricks.

Some people like to add oils or herbs to the water. Some add a silver coin or gemstone to a bowl, cauldron, or cup. These are all acceptable, though they may change the nature of your messages/images.

If you are using a reflective surface like a mirror, you will be able to see your own face — though dimly. Keep gazing at it until the face changes. It may morph into another human-looking face, or it may appear entirely non-human. It is normal for your peripheral vision to darken so that you experience something like tunnel vision. Likewise, it can be part of the process to have moments where your center field of vision goes dark for a short time. All of these changes are temporary, and they are part of your entering the trance state necessary for this work. Stay with it. Keep softly gazing. Watching. Waiting.

You may also experience other physical sensations. Ringing in your ears. Feelings of hot and cold creeping or flashing across your face, neck, or chest. Sudden awareness of aromas. These are all normal. Messages are most likely to come visually with scrying, but it is still very possible to hear or otherwise sense the Spirit. Be open to these other ways of perceiving as you gaze.

Talking Board

Most people know the talking board or Spirit board by one of its most famous brand names — Ouija, a specific board which is a copyrighted design and name held by the Hasbro novelty company. Talking boards far predate the toy and game companies, however. In fact, they have their origins in 1100 AD Chinese culture, where a type of planchette-based automatic writing occurred in a mystic sect. We see talking boards again in a Spiritualist camp in Ohio in 1886, employed in a seance. In both cases, the board was used to communicate with the Dead. In 1890 the first boards were produced by novelty companies, and the public generally viewed them as a harmless parlor game.

That view still exists, of course, along with countless dire warnings about the ill effects of dabbling with the Spirit world through this ultra accessible medium. The warnings aren't wrong on a couple of points:

Talking boards do make Spirit communication easier for both the operator and Spirit.

The board is best left alone by those with little or no occult knowledge and experience.

I heartily disagree that talking boards are "dangerous" or that they are likely to result in "demon possession," as I have heard many people claim. What happens much more often is that folks (usually teenagers) looking for a scare use the board and end up talking with Spirits who are happy to oblige in spooking them. They get prescient and unnerving messages, feel the palpable presence of the Unseen, and perpetuate the myth of the board's terrors.

In reality, the talking board is no more dangerous than a cell phone or the Internet, which are also communication tools. Phones and the Internet do pose some dangers, as we generally agree. Phishing scams, hackers, and all manner of predators try literally every day to access our personal information, steal from us, harm businesses and agencies that we rely on, and even to get real world victims for all sorts of nefarious ends. And yet, we don't see any exhortations that these tools are so inherently evil that we must abandon them entirely. Instead, we practice some precautions, teach new and vulnerable users how to protect themselves, and happily connect with hundreds or thousands of people who only exist for us in an "unseen" and digital form.

Using a talking board is no more dangerous than this. If we use it with some savvy and cunning, we can usually avoid the more unsavory entities who would otherwise be all too happy to take advantage of the naive and foolish among us. And if a harmful Spirit does make contact, we can cut off that communication and send them on their way much like we do when someone spams our phones or social media accounts with sunglasses ads. "Blocking" on a talking board is very possible. We call it banishing.

You'll actually be surprised how infrequently you need to banish these unpleasant or destructive Spirits, if you know how to protect yourself, call on the Spirit world "properly," and know *how* to banish. Most predators (with or without physical bodies) are looking for victims. They rarely want to engage with anyone who puts up a fight or who even looks like they can or would fight.

So how does one properly use a talking board? What precautions or preparations should you make?

Use it in sacred space. Lay your Compass and build the Pyramid. Put the board within the triangle of the Pyramid. As part of this process, ask your Ancestors or the Witch Father or Witch Mother for protection.

Only work the board with a partner you trust. You can absolutely use it by yourself, but if you're going to work with a partner or with spectators present, do so only with your most trusted people.

Don't come to this work hoping, looking, or asking to be titillated and frightened. Check yourself and your motivations. Align the Three Souls ("ground and center") before starting.

Be prepared to banish. Know that you know a sorcerous formula or have tools on hand to send a harmful Spirit away. Your rope and feathers, banishing incense, Venus Water or Florida Water — these are all great.

When you ask for a Spirit to come forward, be clear about what you want to achieve. Either ask for the Spirit by name and have their sigil next to or under the board, or say something like:

"I call into the Unseen and ask for guidance and wisdom from a Spirit who would help me, one with whom I have affinity and who will not seek to harm me."

With these basic practices in place, you should have a rewarding experience using the talking board. Having done the preparatory work, you're ready to engage. (Please note: these preparations apply to all communication tools, really.)

The mechanics of using a talking board are pretty straightforward. The room can be as dark or light as you prefer, but you will need at least enough light to see the letters and numbers on the board clearly. You and your partner (if one is present) will put your fingertips on the planchette. I suggest using only one hand each and recommend the dominant hand. Most planchettes are heart-shaped pieces of wood on little feet that glide easily cross the surface of the board. You'll likely be more comfortable and find that nobody's hand obscures the indicated symbols if you each touch the sides of the planchette, not the point or butt.

I recommend having paper and pen handy. Sometimes Spirits don't spell well. Sometimes they don't even communicate in your preferred language, so it is helpful to be able to jot down strings of letters to sound out the message. I have also used the recorder on my phone in order to review sessions later. In fact, almost all of the talking board sessions initially conducted for the first exploration of the Legion (conducted with my ex) exist as sound files.

Don't be afraid to ask questions and request clarification. This is a dialogue, after all. Some of the common questions from my sessions include:

Who am I speaking with?

What name do you prefer?

What insight do you have for me on [this situation]?

I didn't understand you. Can you try that again?

I don't know what you mean. Can you say it another way?

I often ask lots of questions about the Spirit and their experience, and I asked lots of follow-up questions about their message. Anytime you are negotiating a Compact, you want to be especially involved in making sure you have all of the details. Personalized questions are going to be specific to the situation, so it is impossible to share generalized examples. But I think of it a little like conducting an interview. I follow certain threads and try to get as much detail as possible.

In the beginning, either you or the Spirit may rely more on "yes / no" questions and answers or a handful of symbols. I've mentioned already that "S" used the letter "s" to mean both "yes" and as a self-referential marker. When I would ask "Who am I speaking with?" the planchette slid to the letter "s." Another (non-Goetic) Spirit weaves a bit of French into the mix when we talk on the board, moving between "yes" and the "oui" in "Ouija," especially when she is answering in the affirmative multiple times in a row. (She has even thrown some more complicated French words into our sessions, which invariably sends me to Google Translate.) Some Spirits will even make use of the graphics, if the board is decorated with them, as a way to communicate ideas and feelings. S slides over to the smiling sun when she's amused or very pleased.

Don't be surprised if a Spirit emerges as a Gatekeeper for your Spirit work. This is fairly common. Usually, either a very close Familiar or a Spirit particularly suited to this work will emerge as a facilitator and guardian for you. S does this for me. She is always the first to speak on the board, and she acts as a sort of dispatcher or telephone operator, connecting me with other Spirits directly or relaying their messages. In some cases, she has worked diligently to keep certain Spirits out. This includes the "Do Not Calls" and also other neutral to negative Spirits that she deems a threat.

Funny story: S does not get along particularly well with one of the other Spirits in my Court. I'll call that other Spirit "Jinnie." It got to the point where I could feel Jinnie breaking through in her effort to get my attention, so I told S to let her through so I could hear what she had to say. The first thing Jinnie spelled out on the board (in a rush so fast it was hard to keep up with) was this phrase: "overprotective nanny-goat gatekeeper b****!" (There's no exclamation point on the board, but you could feel the punctuation in her tone.)

When it is clear that a Spirit has stepped into this role for you either at your request or because they volunteered and jumped into the work, you may also notice how they interact with other Witches' Familiars. S is strong and well-suited to this task. If I'm on a talking board with anyone else, S is always the Gatekeeper for the entire session. My ex-wife and I were surprised by that. She could feel and hear her own Gatekeeper Familiar, who was also a Spirit of the Legion; and my ex had engaged in mediumship and been a professional psychic longer than me. It seemed logical that her Familiar would take the lead, but this is just not how it worked out. S always drives.

Your Gatekeeper will be an important ally for you in this work. They will make communication with other Spirits easier, and they will offer you a first layer of protection against Spirits who mean you harm.

Note: the Gatekeeper role for Familiars isn't specific to using talking boards. They're present and active for all types of Spirit work. I only mentioned their function here because it was while using the board that I initially became aware of my own Gatekeeper.

Pendulum

Because I don't love the mechanics of using a board and planchette for solo work, I switched out the planchette for a pendulum and use the board as a pendulum chart. Later I made a mat that was more user friendly with the pendulum.

I admit to finding it amusing that our culture has developed such fear around the talking board, but basic pendulum divinations are common even among Christian folk. Pregnant women often use a crucifix necklace to determine the sex of their unborn baby by letting it swing over their bellies. Straight lines mean male. Circles mean female.

A pendulum can be created by suspending any type of weight (or "plumb") from a string. Many pendulums are made from semi-precious stones, shells, woods, and metals that were chosen due to their alignments with particular energies. However, you can use any combination of materials that resonates with you. Indeed, a necklace with a pendant or heavy charm that you wear daily may serve as your truest pendulum, as it is already attuned to your energy.

When you wish to use your pendulum for divination, start by holding it in your dominant hand. It helps to put your elbow on a table or hold it close to your side to minimize your movement. Still your mind with a few breaths and then ask the pendulum to show you YES, then show you NO. Make note of the types of swings. For some people, these will always be the same, every time you ask. It is important to begin with this simple exercise, however, because the energy of other individuals (including Spirits) can occasionally change the direction of your pendulum's movements — which would change everything about the reading you conduct. From here, you can conduct a "reading" by asking Yes/No questions.

A pendulum reading can also be conducted using a semi-circular "mat" or "board" drawn on paper, wood, leather, or cloth onto which you have inscribed letters, numbers, names, symbols, or other information you wish the pendulum to indicate. This can be very elaborate and can extend the usefulness of your pendulum into many different areas beyond Yes/No questions. I've included some examples of pendulum mats at the end of this chapter that can be used in combination with your pendulum just as they are, in fact.

Pendulums, I find, tend to be one of our inspirited tools. That is to say that a pendulum often has a Spirit of its own indwelling within it, separate from your Gatekeeper. The pendulum Spirit is not usually as vocal as your Gatekeeper, though. If you work a lot with pendulums, you will notice that different ones have different personalities and skills. For example, some are better suited to conversations about love and relationship, while others act as job coaches, giving us clear insight into our work and purpose in the world. Thank your pendulum verbally, make offerings, etc.

Spirit Writing

While some people are inclined to automatic writing without any prior mediumship training, I found for myself that I needed a little experience, mostly so I could trust what I was hearing was from Spirit.

For me, using this tool was something of an extension of two other practices:

1) using a pendulum with a lettered chart

2) journaling

Because I'm so verbal by nature, I found that I was "hearing" messages as they came through the pendulum, and a similar thing would happen when I journaled.

In fact, I usually refer to this particular practice as "Spirit Writing" or "Spirit Journaling" and not "automatic writing," which is a common term for it and similar practices. With pure or classic automatic writing, though, a Medium is often unaware of what their hand is writing. The Medium holds a pen to paper, but they don't look at the markings while they engage in some other cognitive activity, like holding a conversation with a person in the room. It is only when they stop and look at the writing that they get an inkling of the message.

That method is great, and you can certainly use it with the Lemegeton, if you do well with it. However, I feel that what I share here as "Spirit Writing" is a little more accessible and just as valid. Indeed, it is the practice I have used for updating almost all of the Spirit descriptions in this 2021 edition of the *Witches' Key to the Legion*.

To engage in Spirit Writing, you just need paper and a pen/cil — although I fully recommend practicing this technique from inside your Compass, with the writing materials in the Pyramid, and sigils, candles, and incense all engaged. If you're new to the process or the Spirit being contacted is unfamiliar to you, the full ritual preparations will make it easier for the Spirit to manifest and for you to get solid messages from them.

The process itself is simple. You'll initiate the session by writing a question or declaration to the Spirit you are contacting, and you continue by immediately writing down <u>any</u> words you hear/

SAMPLE OF SPIRIT WRITING FROM ONE OF MY JOURNALS

think in reply. If you relax into the process, you may be surprised how distinctly the voice of the "Other" is in your mind. Try not to fight it, question it, or overthink this process too much. Tell your internal editor to take the night off while you exchange notes with the Spirit.

There are a lot of processes at work here that make this method so effective. One is that the act of writing words out mechanically takes time and concentration from one part of your brain, which frees up another part of your brain for hearing this "Other" that speaks directly to your psyche. You end up taking dictation for Spirit, in essence.

Can it work with typing instead of handwriting? I'm sure for some people it can. A lot of it depends on how fluently and rapidly you type, as well as how much you have come to recognize and trust the messages that come from that other place within you.

I have a personal preference for the handwritten practice of Spirit Writing for a few reasons. One, is that it lets me feel the energy a of the interaction a little better without having an electronic device in the mix. I would really never take my laptop into ritual space with me, but a journal and pen are longtime magickal companions.

Another is that handwriting the messages feels more personal, as if I am writing love letters or engaging in correspondence with a penpal. Also, there are times when the message coming through is a symbol or picture that I can draw or sketch, but I would be distracted and taken pretty far out of the moment to break out graphics/drawing software to accomplish the same thing with a computer or tablet. (Hardcore artists like my friend John who contributed so many amazing illustrations to this book might have a very different experience, though. I know for a fact that much of his work is completed while in Spirit contact, and he often works digitally, with stunning, Spirit-filled results.)

Finally, there are so many times when part of the message has actually been communicated in the difference between my handwriting and the Spirit's script. There is often a different weight and lilt to the lettering, and so much of their tone, personality, and mood has been conveyed this way for me, that I wouldn't know how to recreate that in a typing scenario.

The session progresses like a conversation, often with questions and answers on both sides, maybe some deal-making or advice-giving, some insight-sharing, and sometimes things like flirting, gossip, comfort, or even scolding. It ends when the Spirit has nothing left to say for now, or when you are too tired to keep going. Sometimes I can hear/feel that a Spirit has more too share, but I am drained from the chat. It isn't always depleting to your personal energy stores to communicate this way, but there are certain factors that can make it tiring — your connection with the Spirit, whether or not you have a strong Compact already, the strength of your Gatekeeper, the Gatekeeper's relationship/affinity with the Spirit you're talking to, the weight and import of the message being conveyed, and of course your own physical health and energy levels prior to the session. I haven't done a thorough study of it, but I would also suspect that planetary alignment and moon phase could have a significant impact on the ease or difficulty of conversations with Spirits. Contacting Spirits during times when they are stronger (or when your own Gatekeeper is) would make it much less necessary for you to expend your own personal energy to make the connection with the Spirit.

One fantastic benefit of Spirit Writing is that you have a record of your communications with Spirits. The journals into which you have these dialogues are treasure troves of insight for you for the rest of your life.

Flying Ointment

Flying ointment is one of the traditional potions of witchcraft. It is the salve used by Witches to induce hallucinations and astral journeying (their method of "flying" to Sabbat). Unfortunately, the recipes for flying ointment in the old grimoires are full of extremely poisonous herbal ingredients. In order to achieve anything but the mildest of psychic "nudges" from those plants, you must literally risk death. This (mostly) non-toxic flying ointment is a Witch salve with KICK. It is not a subtle brew! Infused with nine herbs (eight in dry plant form; one as essential oil), each of which is known for its psychic/journeying properties, this ointment will "knock you into next Tuesday."

4 ounces Olive Oil

1 ounce Beeswax, grated

1 ounce Honey, raw

2 tablespoons Mugwort

2 tablespoons Cinquefoil

2 tablespoons Lemongrass

1 tablespoon Rue

1 tablespoon Dittany of Crete

1 tablespoon Balm of Gilead

1 tablespoon Wormwood

1 tablespoon Calamus root

2 drops Clary Sage essential oil (add after the mixture has been strained)

A salve (or ointment) is made when a warm infused oil is mixed with beeswax or plant-butters to harden into a soft cream for topical applications to the skin.

Materials Needed:

Crockpot/ slow cooker

Glass jars with lids

Grater

Containers (tins, jars, etc)

Cheesecloth, pillowcase, or strainer

Dried herbs

Start by making an infused oil:

Fill a jar (or multiple jars) 1/2 full with the herbs of your choice. Cover the herbs with olive oil and stir to release air bubbles. Cap the jars and place on a towel in slow cooker. Fill with water to oil line of the jars. Heat on the lowest setting for 8-10 hours, gently shaking the jars every couple of hours. Strain the herbs from the oil. (You can compost the plant matter.)

Add hardening agents to make salve:

Grate the beeswax (or cocoa/shea butter) and add it with the honey into the warm infused oil. If you have allowed the oil to cool, you can always grate the wax and melt it prior to mixing it into the oil. The more wax you use, the harder the salve will be when it is cooled. For a softer salve, use a ratio of 1 part beeswax, 1 part honey, and 4 parts oil. This firmness "gives" without being too hard, but it isn't sticky. It melts nicely on the skin. Pour the well-blended mix into clean, airtight containers. Cap, label, and allow to cool. Store in a cool, dark cabinet.

To use, take a three-finger scoop and rub it on until the skin is warm. Apply it to pulse points such as the neck, the wrists, the underarms, the inner thighs & the feet. The scent is intoxicating and smells different on the skin than in the jar. Give it about 15 minutes and begin focusing on "flying out." It works well just before bedtime to produce lucid dreams, and (as it was designed) it's ideal for an aid to astral travel, especially visions of flying out on a riding pole. Guided meditations benefit favorably from the use of a smaller dose. It combines well with other entheogens also. My Coven has used it with excellent results with Sabbat Wine.

Sabbat Wine

Sabbat Wine is the name of a group of entheogens used by Witches to induce an ecstatic or altered state during rituals. Flying Ointment is sometimes called Sabbat Wine, although many modern Witches make a mulled wine that is sometimes drunk in addition to applying Flying Ointment. This Sabbat Wine blend is suitable for occasional use, such as initiations or special oracle rituals. For more frequent consumption, consider replacing the mugwort with another herb, as mugwort can build up in your liver if drunk too often.

2 parts Mugwort

1 part Lemongrass

Steep 1 tsp of the above mixture in 1 cup of warmed sweet red wine. Add raw, local honey to taste.

The mugwort and lemongrass blend is a very effective, albeit bitter, tea. The bitterness of the herbs works well with a particularly sweet red wine and a little local honey.

Drink a cup or two of the Sabbat Wine before flying out, performing possessory rituals, or holding initiations.

Pendulum Mat 1

Pendulum Mat 2

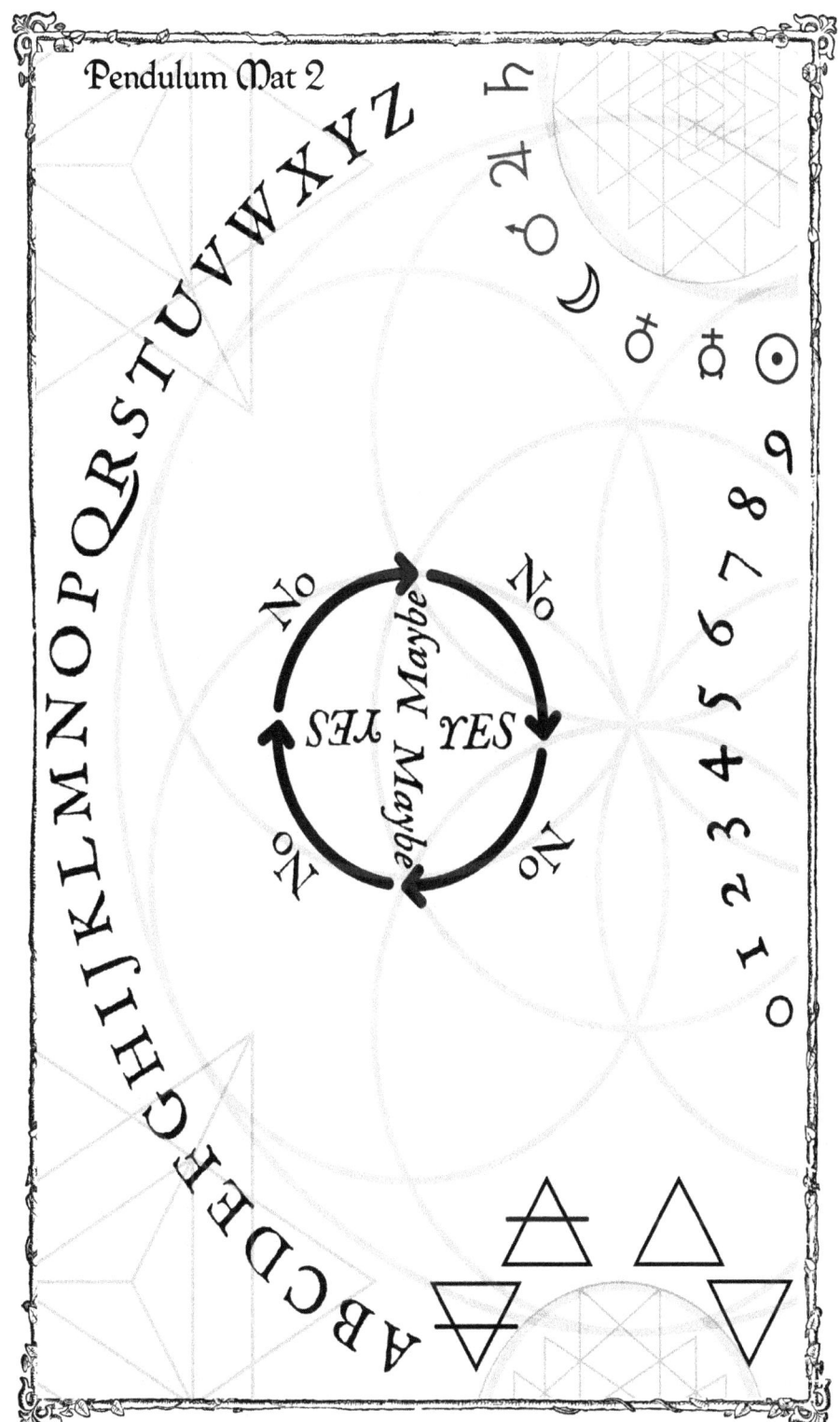

The Compact

It could be reasonably argued that there is a bargain at play between the Witch and every Familiar Spirit with whom they work. Some bargains are made explicitly and formally ("I'll do this for you if you do that for me"), while others are implied or assumed. In the latter case, what each party is receiving may be unclear or unspoken, but it is likely there. In *The Clovenstone Workings*, Robin Artisson suggests that in such cases, the Witch can look to the nature of their dreams for clues regarding what the Spirit is getting as their part of the bargain. Perhaps they feed on excess psychic energy or engage with you in a satisfying way in the Land of Dreams.

The relationship between Witch and Spirit is described in folkloric texts (like the trial records of accused 13th to 18th Century Witches) as being both hereditary and deal-based. Witches often inherited Spirits along family lines, and the Spirit generally expected "care and feeding" for services rendered. That care and feeding typically looked like the provision of a Spirit vessel or house of some sort (which we cover in the next chapter, "The Vessel") and offerings (which we will talk about in the chapter following that). It was beyond rare, in these classic examples, for a Spirit to attach themselves to a Witch and perform feats of healing, hexing, prophecy, weather manipulation, or any other blessing or bane without receiving something in return.

I would argue that it is still rare for a Spirit to engage with a Witch or Mage without some benefit to themselves. However, I would add the caveat that sometimes those benefits are subtle enough not to be easily discernible by the Witch — and in a few unfortunate cases, the Spirits may be intentionally devious so as to evade the Witch's notice. (The latter has too often been the case with the Spirits on the "Do Not Call" list, which is one of the reasons my Spirits and I advocate so heartily against calling them.)

In order to avoid this sort of vague and lopsided relationship in which you find yourself owing a debt that you may not be prepared to pay, it is a custom of the Wise to make the contract explicit right from the start. There are so many ways you can approach this, and a great deal will depend on your sense of Arte, the Spirits with whom you regularly communicate, and what you are trying to accomplish.

I'd like to suggest a few things to consider:

1. If you aren't sure where to start, consider making an offer. If you have a task that needs to be done, a role in your Spirit Court that needs to be filled, or something else on your mind, you can propose both your need and a specific offering to a Spirit to get the thing done. Think of this as akin to posting a job description with a salary expectation. From here, the Spirit might negotiate a slightly different payment before settling on terms, but it gives you a starting place.

2. You can approach a single Spirit in isolation to see if they want to work with you on your concern, or you can make the offer to a group of Spirits with attributes in common with whom you might have affinity and then see who is most eager to respond. I could make equally valid arguments for the politeness of both approaches. The first one gives a Spirit ample individual time to consider the deal, while the second one means that the Spirit who answers the call never falls into a "second or third choice" category.

3. Get specific in your wording of the Compact (the bargain/agreement/deal) between you and the Spirit. Write it down so you are clear on it in the future. Include descriptions that indicate amount, intensity, frequency, and duration of the offering, if applicable.

4. Don't rule out an offering because it seems too "weird" —

or not weird enough. We'll talk more about this in the chapter on offerings, but the truth is that anything goes. As long as you are comfortable giving it (for the duration, intensity, frequency, etc. to which you've agreed), then it is fine.

5. Uphold your end of the deal. The Spirit is giving you something, and you are beholden to reciprocate. Faltering on your end of the deal could see that which is given taken away again, turned on you, and your ability to deal effectively now and in the future with other Spirits weakened. If what you have been given is something that is woven deeply into your life, you will surely feel its loss on a deep level.

6. Sign the Compact by seal and blood. Mark your own bindrune or sigil as well as that of the Spirit along with 1, 3, or 9 drops of your blood on the paper on which you wrote out your Compact. Fold this into a packet, tie it with red string, and keep it in a safe container among your magickal things.

The Vessel

One of the common elements that we see in researching or observing Spirit work among traditional or folkloric practices is the use of a container, house, or vessel for the Spirit to use as a dwelling place in the physical plane. Let's look at some examples of where this happens, why we think it is needed on a metaphysical level, and how we can implement it in our own work.

Spirit Vessels -- A Cross-Cultural Phenomena

Since the timelines of these sorcerous expressions overlap and undoubtedly intermingled with each other at various crossroads, I'm presenting them here in no particular order of either chronology or significance.

Solomonic/Grimoire Tradition: The classical grimoires and books of demonolatry (including the Lemegeton, or Ars Goetia, the Lesser Key of Solomon) usually favor and are very explicit about the use of containers for holding and binding a Spirit. The belief in these grimoires was that Spirits would do the Conjurer harm if they were free to operate on their accord after having been summoned to the physical plane. In order to control the Spirit, and protect the Conjurer, a metal vessel much like a spoutless samovar in appearance was employed. The vessel was engraved with binding charms and formulas in magickal scripts.

African Diasporic Tradition: Coming from New Orleans and Haitian Voudon as well as the African Traditional Religions of West Africa (like Dahomey, Congo, and others), we see often elaborately decorated bottles used to house a number of Spirits. These are often glass bottles, with cobalt being the preferred color -- through amber, green, rose, and other colored glasses have their own meanings and uses. Spirits who might dwell within such a bottle include Ancestors, Lwa, animals, and local land Spirits. The bottles are often (but not always) decorated to honor the Spirit inside, using shells, beads, seeds, tassles, braids, ribbons, doll parts (heads/arms), feathers, bones, and more. Some bottles from ADT practices are intended to capture and bind Spirits (against their wills), but others are intended as places of comfort, rest, and offering.

European Folkloric Tradition: Trial records, nursery rhymes, and fairy tales give us a lot of insight into how Spirits of all sorts were housed within European folk custom. Some (like Beelzibub and Trullibub, who came to Elizabeth Chandler) were content to dwell in a log and a twig, respectively. Others asked for or were given jars, boxes, baskets, and other common household containers. These were often filled with objects for the comfort, entertainment, and work of the Spirit, such as fabric scraps, broken or cast-off tools, spell ingredients, etc. The Grimm fairytale of "The Spirit in the Bottle" ("Der Geist im Glas") echoes of the Arabic folkloric tales "Aladdin and the Magic Lamp" and the "Fisherman and the Jinni," and remind us how enduring and far-reaching the idea of Spirits trapped in household containers may be.

Southeast Asian Traditions: In Burma, Cambodia, Thailand, Malaysia, Laos, Indonesia, and the Philippines, Spirit houses are miniature houses mounted on a pedestal or dais where offerings are made to the Spirits who inhabit the area. These could be animal Spirits, Ancestors, local land Spirits, etc. These Spirits are propitiated to keep their good favor and prevent them from causing trouble for the people who live nearby.

Why Do Spirits Need a Vessel?

Strictly speaking, a Spirit doesn't require a vessel, house, or any type of physical encasement in order to operate on the physical plane. Chances are good for many practitioners that they have interacted positively with Spirits that had no such dwelling. However, when we have evoked Spirits from the realms of the Unseen, which are more aerial and less corporeal than our own, we are asking them to be more present with us in this Seen World, this Green World of life and substance and physical being. It is often easier and more comfortable for them to do so if we give them a physical "thing" to occupy.

I think of it much like offering them a body. Indeed, sometimes the vessels we see in folkloric examples are dolls (which are often fabric, clay, wood, or paper *bodies* of human or animal shapes). Even if the vessel is house-shaped (or bottle- or jar- or log- or jewelry-shaped) and not fashioned at all like a body, it still serves much the same purpose. It is a sanctuary that the Spirit can choose to occupy while in the Green World, and it provides them an interface for experiencing sensation and receiving offerings.

It is to (or within/on top of, etc) this vessel that we are going to provide the food, drinks, incense smoke, anointing oils, or other offerings that the Spirit prefers. They will "consume" it in their own way, which will of course look different than when a living human consumes the same. Cakes will dry out and become hard. Liquors will evaporate and form a thick syrup. Smoke will swirl, and we may never see the nose that sniffs the sweetened air, but we can be sure that the Spirit has taken it to themselves in their way.

What I can't recommend is using these vessels as a way to capture and imprison wandering Spirits, later compelling them to do your bidding. I always advocate building reciprocal relationships with Spirits, so it is best if we forgo the (yes, once traditional) enslavement practices utilized by our forebears. (They felt like this was an acceptable way to treat people, as well. Abandoning such practices in favor of cooperation and partnership is one small part of decolonizing our magick -- a topic I covered in the November 2020 issue of *ev0ke*.)

Spirit Vessels in Your Craft

Some Spirits are very communicative and will tell you right away what they want and need in a vessel. One of my primarily Familiars ("S"), told me she wanted a blue jar. I found an iridescent blue ceramic sugar bowl on my next trip to the local flea market, and I could practically hear her giggling with delight. My daughter's primary Familiar told her in a talking board session that he wanted her to repurpose a little painted wooden house that she had decorated and adorned for a plush frog that had come with said house as part of a set. He said, "I been lookin' at you' frog house," and with that he claimed the space. She just needed to paint his symbol over the door to make it his.

Other Spirits can either be less particular or less vocal, which means you may have to rely on your own instincts more, go with something that speaks to you, or wait longer until you have enough signs and indicators to feel comfortable moving ahead with the project.

As far as what shape that vessel might take, what materials you might use, or what your process might look like -- all these things depend on the desires of your Spirit and your own sense of the Arte. For some of us, it just isn't Witchcraft if we don't get deeply crafty -- collecting clay from a local river bed and sculpting it into a bowl engraved with the sigils of our Familiar. For others, an unadorned colored bottle picked up from the discount dishware is magickal enough, as long as our Familiar is happy with it.

Some vessel options to consider: birdhouse, dollhouse, colored bottles, canning jars, decorative perfume bottles, decanters, vases, urns, amphoras, dolls of all sorts, wood carvings, trinket boxes, cigar boxes, clasped chests, lockets, rings, pendants, oil lamps (ancient and contemporary), lanterns, candles, animal skulls, bones. The options here are really endless.

Whatever you choose, you should add some type of embellishment to mark it as belonging to your Spirit. Even a small change can have a major impact. For this, you might include: engraving or painting the sigil or bindrune of the Spirit, adding flowers, seeds, beads, coins, braids, tassels, feathers, doll head/arms, teeth, claws, bones, fur, wood, stones, etc.

A FEW SPIRIT VESSELS -- SUGAR BOWL, CANE TOAD POUCH, WICKER BUNNY BASKET, TIARA

Offerings

There are three main types of offering we are going to cover as part of Goetic workings for Witches — the offerings that are part of your Spirit Compact, the offertory meal that is typically included at the end of each ritual, and the other incidental offerings that you may need to make here and there.

Spirit Compact Offerings

Honestly, there is endless variety when it comes to the type of offerings that might be included in the deals and bargains you make. These are the things you give to or do for the Spirit in order to "feed" them energy in return for what they give to or do for you. Some examples might include:

- Blending and burning a specific incense
- Keeping an anointed candle lit
- Placing 7 drops of your blood on a stone and burying it during every full moon
- Energetic/psychic sex with the Spirit
- Crafting a Spirit doll in their likeness and carrying it with you wherever you go
- Saying "Thank you, [Spirit]" every time you hear or see a specific signal
- Posting art embedded with the Spirit's sigil on your social media account once per week

You're only limited by three things when it comes to offerings: your creativity (in terms of what you can think of as a possible way to honor or feed your Spirit), the Spirit's willingness to accept a specific offering, and your willingness to provide it once it has been brought to your attention as an otherwise viable option.

There are certainly offerings that are more traditional than others. Blood, food, drink (especially milk and liquor), and sexual energy are among the most potent of these. Interestingly, blood and sexual energy also draw a pretty strong reaction from most people (even other magickal practitioners) when they are mentioned as offerings.

And why is that? Well, all four of these represent vital life force — those things that sustain us. We need food and drink to survive, and liquor has long been considered a gift from the Gods to ease the hardship of life and open a pathway to the Mysteries. Blood and sex, though, are those life-sustaining forces that we produce and harbor within our own bodies — and that hold tremendous power. They are easy to access, easy to unleash, and easy to abuse if not respected. There is a powerful combination at play here (the body, the balance of Life and Death, enormous power) that has made blood and sex taboo.

I'm going to go ahead and note that milk (which also comes from the body and is vitally sustaining for at least very young humans) is indeed a potent offering to many Spirits, but doesn't carry the taboos of blood and sex. (Although one could argue that there are currently social taboos around human breastmilk that put it in an "off-limits" sort of category for most people. This serves to highlight its intimate, life-sustaining, and valuable nature.)

If you're looking for your most traditional offerings, these would be my recommendations, along with wine, honey, and a few resins like copal, frankincense, and myrrh.

The Red Meal

A great number of religious, magickal, and mystical traditions share in common a sacrificial or eucharistic meal as part of their canon of rites. Witchcraft is no exception, and we see variations of this meal in both Wiccan and non-Wiccan expressions of the Craft.

Regardless of the tradition of Witchcraft you practice, it is very likely that you already have and use a "Housle" or "Cakes and Ale" ceremony. In terms of a Goetic practice such as we are embracing here, it is helpful to think of this ceremony (which in my own tradition is often referred to as the Red Meal, due to the sacrificial nature of its constituent parts) as an offertory meal shared by all of the incarnate and discarnate participants in the ritual. Whereas you might normally think of it as only for the Godds or the Ancestors and yourself, it is important to offer a portion of the bread and wine to the Spirit(s) with whom you communicated or otherwise worked during this rite.

The Red Meal or Housle can be offered without words, of course, or you can use those that come spontaneously to you. I've included a full copy of the Spiral Castle Tradition's ceremony for your reference at the end of this chapter.

Just be sure to bring food and drink for this portion of the ritual working when you prepare for ritual. It serves the purpose of saying "thank you" to those Spirits who attended you, and it also will help to ground you as the ritual is ending.

Incidental Offerings

Sometimes you'll call a Spirit with whom you have never worked before (or maybe they volunteer themselves through your Gatekeeper), and you'll engage in a communication session. This isn't a Spirit with whom you have a working arrangement, and maybe they aren't hanging around long after this one ritual. Even so, they might ask for a token of favor or a small payment for this little bit of "freelance work." Then again, they may not ask, but maybe you'd rather give them a specific payment for services rendered — just to be sure there is no bill to be paid later.

This is just one example of how such an "incidental" offering might come about. In a case like this, you might give an offering from a selection of things you keep on-hand. It could be handy to keep certain resins, a jar of honey, a lancet (Red Knife/thumb-pricker) around for easy blood-drawing, or a few white utility candles for fixing and dressing in a Spirit's honor.

The Red Meal

Moving counterclockwise, bring the sacrificial meal to the Stang or center of the Compass, while singing the Housle Song, below. Make at least one full circle as you tread the mill. Three is better.

The Housle Song

(To the tune of Greensleeves)

> *To Housle now we walk the wheel*
> *We kill tonight the blood red meal*
> *A leftward tread of magick's mill*
> *To feed the Godds and work our Will.*
>
> *Red! Red is the wine we drink!*
> *Red! Red are the cords we wear!*
> *Red! Red is the blood of Godd!*
> *And red is the shade of the Housle*

Say, *"For my Ancestors, my Godds, the Spirits, and Myself, I do this."*

Bless the bread with your right hand by saying: "Here is bread, flesh of the Earth, blessed to give us life and strength. I consecrate it in the name of the Old Ones."

Kill the bread by saying: "I take its life and give it to Them." Cut it with the red knife using your left hand.

Bless the wine with your right hand by saying: "Here is wine, blood of the Earth, blessed to give us joy and abundance. I consecrate it in the name of the Old Ones."

Kill the wine by saying: "I take its life and give it to Them." Slide the knife over the top of the cup to cut its throat, using your left hand.

Eat and drink of the Meal, making whatever personal offerings you like into the bowl.

The remainder of the wine is poured into the bread bowl. Dip your finger in and anoint yourself. This can also be used for blessing and saining tools, etc.

The Meal is either given to the ground now (if outside) or later (if inside) with the following Declaration:

"By the Red, and Black and White,
Light in Darkness, Dark in Light --
What we take, we freely give.
We all must die. We all must live.
Above, below, and here are One.
All together -- ALL! (And none!)
Here is shown a Mystery. As I Will, so Mote it Be."

In Case of Emergency

It is my sincere hope that you never find yourself in a situation where you need to use what I might call "nuclear options" for protecting yourself from a Spirit with whom you are communicating. My training, experience, and observation tell me that if you come into a Goetic practice prepared with the skillset and toolkit we've already discussed and don't fool around with the Spirits on the "Do Not Call" list, you should be fine.

However, I can foresee a few circumstances in which you might need to go to greater lengths to dissuade a Spirit away from their fixation on you. Perhaps, for instance, you are dealing with a particularly nasty Spirit who isn't mentioned in this collection. There are certainly plenty of other daemons mentioned in other classical grimoires, and this current work is not positioned to comment on whether or not you should call all of them. Similarly, you might have started a dialogue with (or otherwise gotten the attention of) one of the eight that I have flagged here before you were warned away from them.

When my (ex-)partner and I started engaging in the Spirit communications that ultimately led to this book, we and our Covenmates came under attack from the Spirits on that list. We found ourselves primarily (and brutally) assaulted in dreams. It didn't happen right away, actually. It only started as we began to take the list seriously — and as I became determined to write the first edition of this book.

I hesitate to describe the attack in writing in any detail to a public audience. I feel that gives the entities who carried it out more fuel. What I will say is that it was:

- Coordinated — Several of us had similar dreams over a 2-3 night span that involved strikingly similar actions and figures

- Horrific — The actions done to us (before we were able to take back control in the dream, for those of us who did) were brutally violent and painfully humiliating. They were torturous on every level.

- Concrete — There was no saving grace of esoteric symbolism underlying the dream imagery. Trust me, I've tried to find it — and I have a poet's heart, so I'd really like for it to be there. But these experiences weren't symbolic or figurative.

- Lucid — More than most dreams, we felt like we were there, present, in a whole sense. Some of us were able to use the lucidity of walking in this Dreamtime to be able to help ourselves. I launched into a Star Ruby (which we'll discuss in a moment), and found that SUPER effective.

I share these descriptive points in part to give you an insight as to why I still advocate against calling the Spirits on the "Do Not Call" list — because at the mere threat of a Witch like me saying, "Hey, friends, of all the 72, don't mess around with these eight," they launched a mob-style hit on my Coven. And also in part to let you know that I have been through something pretty traumatic related to my Spirit work — and here I am, still doing the work. Trust me, that wouldn't be the case if I didn't have both faith and proof that I could put a stop to situations like the one that I described.

Back in the chapter dealing with "Cleansing, Shielding, and Banishing," I offered lots of great tools and suggestions for both cleansing and banishing that can be applied even in your trickiest, toughest situations. Typically, you'll use them in some sort of combination for a big problem — an emergency. Think "Bell, Book, and Candle" — vibration, formula/words of power, and light, used together or in rapid succession.

Florida Water paired with your black-handled knife are also a powerful combination for compelling a Spirit to leave your space. Typically, when I have done this, I have sprayed a bit of the Florida Water our of my mouth (yeah, it doesn't taste great), cut an X with the edge of my blade, and pushed out with the flat of my blade. I do this first in the direction in which I perceive the Spirit, and then at the Gates/Quarters all around. If a situation arises outside the Compass, I do this at the windows, outer doors, and mirrors.

I mentioned earlier that when I was under attack in my sleep (and this happened once from the "Do Not Calls" and once from another practitioner who had a bit of a snap and targeted me online and off), I rather instinctively launched into performing the Star Ruby ritual. If you aren't familiar with the Star Ruby, it is an adaptation of the Lesser [Banishing] Ritual of the Pentagram. The LBRP originated with the Hermetic Order of the Golden Dawn (based, according to the Order's lore, on ancient rituals), and Crowley is responsible for the Star Ruby adaptation. Of the two, I've always really resonated with the Star Ruby — most likely because I get to speak Greek throughout the whole thing (with the exception of a few names).

There is a copy of what my Tradition calls the "Witches' LBRP" in the section on Cleansing, Shielding, and Banishing. This is an adaptation of the traditional LBRP with a couple of nods to the Star Ruby. It's purposes are ostensibly the same as these older rituals that are foundational within the world of Ceremonial Magick and Thelema. As Graham John Wheeler wrote in <u>Correspondences Journal</u> in 2020, the LBRP is used so that one "may have protection against opposing forces, and also that they may form some idea of how to attract and to come into communication with spiritual and invisible things." Practitioners are encouraged to perform the ritual daily to better achieve those ends. We have also discussed already that it can be used prior to ritual or magickal workings, and I would suggest that I have seen it (or a variation) used to clear and reset the space when something has gone amiss — even dreadfully so. In fact, a slightly shook (and maybe a little ticked off) Witch reclaiming their space with a forceful LBRP (Witchy or Hermetic) or Star Ruby is a fearsome sight!

After you've done the in-the-moment banishing to remove the Spirit from the space, you need to take steps to prevent their return. Follow banishing with blessing and warding the space, yourself, and what/whomever needs to be protected. Bless with Angel Water and/or a Consecration Incense. (Frankincense, myrrh, and copal are fantastic for blessing, if you want to use something simple.) Create a new or additional protection ladder. Carry a protective amulet or design and empower a talisman to protect you. It's important not to leave yourself vulnerable to a repeat of the incident.

To that end, it's important to do some analysis of WHY this happened. It can be too tempting to think, "I'm just a magnet for negative Spirits," or "I can't control this." I'm going to be a little harsh here and say that if you genuinely believe that, deep down, then you should stay away from Spirit work — and maybe away from the Craft. If you feel yourself to be out of control, you are. If you believe you draw big, negative psychic experience and spiritual encounters, I can promise you that you will draw them time and again if you keep putting yourself in their path.

Please don't mistake what I'm saying with spiritual bypassing and victim-blaming. I really detest the toxic positivity that pervades so much of the current spiritual landscape (including Neo-Paganism and Witchcraft). I do not believe that negative experiences are the fault of the person who had them — that they brought them on themselves somehow. In general, I find the "blame game" to be pretty fruitless and destructive — and toxic.

What I do believe is that effects have causes, and we can't hope to mitigate those causes if we don't know what they are. And we can't possibly know what the causes are if we throw our hands up in the air in hapless impotence — or worse, indulge in the "specialness" of being "incurably afflicted by the Spirit World."

This second variation, I call "Munchausen's by Pixie." If Munchausen's Syndrome is a psychological condition whereby the afflicted person makes themselves physically ill in order to get sympathy and attention, and "Munchausen's by Proxy" is where they make someone close to them ill, then "Munchausen's by Pixie" is my tongue-in-cheek way of describing the very real phenomena in which we see folks who are routinely being possessed by Spirits and ridden by Godds without consent, attacked by Unseen assailants, and generally haunted, hexed, and tormented — despite having been provided with assistance, guidance, and tools that have been proven effective across time and cultures. If you've been involved in the occult or Craft community, you've likely met an individual who is dealing with this.

There is hope! I've seen more than one person have a "Come to Lucifer" enlightenment moment and turn this mindset around. If this has been you — constantly plagued by the Unseen — consider this a (mostly) gentle and entirely private call out. Start by asking yourself three difficult and thorny questions.

1) "Is it possible that I am having psychotic or hallucinatory episodes associated with a mental illness?" If you've been previously diagnosed with a condition that is connected to hallucinations and delusions, please explore this thoroughly. Believe me when I say that medication to help control the negative hallucinations/delusions will not make you any less powerful or attuned as a Witch. I know so many Witches who are dealing with exactly these issues, and it is very possible to see into the Other Worlds and learn to reality test and differentiate between true spiritual visions and illness-induced hallucinations.

2) "What benefits do I get from my present Spirit/psychic-torment?" Don't just say "none." Consider whether or not members of your community rush to your aid when you have a problem. Maybe they are people you view as leaders, teachers, or elders. Maybe they are people who you think might not be very interested in you if it weren't for your problems, which they are uniquely qualified to handle. Or maybe there is a rush of adrenaline when a new problem pops up — like the plunge on a roller coaster or jump scare on a haunted house. Similarly, you might cherish the dopamine or oxytocin flood of being comforted after a negative experience. Those are powerful chemicals in the body and brain, and we can get addicted to them — even when we might have something like embarrassment or shame around the idea of causing a scene in a group ritual or seeming overly dramatic (again) among people that have been through this with us before. There may be other things buried in the experience for you — reminders or re-enactments of past traumas, for example. Whatever you're "getting" isn't likely to be purely positive, which is why you've probably not recognized it as a benefit until now.

3) "What could I gain by committing to a thorough banishing practice?" If you made the changes (took the meds, did the therapy, embraced the various cleansing, shielding, and banishing tools described here or taught to you by those same elders/teachers/leaders who have tried to help), your relationship with Spirit would be transformed and your life would lose a LOT of its drama. I don't know your life, so I don't know how dramatic it is right now; but if you are experiencing the level of psychic distress and spiritual torment I described, it's a pretty safe bet that you've probably got some distress happening in other areas, too. Just cutting out this one area of stress and anxiety would free you up to deal with those other things. And — from my experience

and observation — you would be developing habits of mind and Soul that might change your appetite and tolerance for the drama, in general. THIS is part of what is meant when the Golden Dawn says the LBRP "protects against impure magnetism" and helps to "get rid of obsessing or disturbing thoughts." I daresay a lot of us (especially in this social media age) have developed an unhealthy dependence on conflict. Humans have always loved bloody and brutal contests of both words and swords — from debates to gladiators to daytime talk shows to cable news. And now divisive, combative argumentation is the primary mode of engagement on many of the social platforms we use to communicate. It's so important that we find some techniques for unlatching from the toxic umbilicus that this contemporary world is trying to keep us linked to. So, with this question, start to imagine life on the other side of the turmoil — and embrace it by taking the steps to truly get there.

And there you have it! This is my basic formula for handling the psychic and Spirit-based emergencies:

Banish—Bless—Protect

and

Pair Magickal and Mundane Approaches

THE SPIRITS OF THE LEGION

Index of Spirits

The pages that follow are filled with practical and esoteric information about each of the 72 Spirits of the Lemegeton. I have pulled as much as I could from the descriptions of these Spirits in the classical grimoires. Many of those grimoires are available in the public domain, but some just give lists of Spirits (sometimes in hierarchies) without any further notation about their attributes. I've done very little editing between the descriptions in order to highlight the varied ways similar features of these Spirits have been described over the centuries.

Also, it's worth noting that I've included some names and descriptions that aren't always attributed to Goetic Spirits by others who research and work with these 72. For example, in *The Book of Oberon*, Fersone, Gorsyar, and Garsone all share a remarkable resemblance to Purson (Corson), so I have included parts of their descriptions in Purson's entry. These may indeed all be Purson, or they may be lesser-known Spirits under Purson's "command" or tutelage. I've tried to be clear in my own notations so you can let your experience of the Spirit, your own research, and your best instincts act as a guide.

A scholar of demonology and Spirit work will know that some of the texts referenced in these descriptions are found in what might generously be called fragmentary (or even borderline legendary) manuscripts. The *Liber Officiorum Spirituum*, just as one example, is referenced in Johann Weyer's *Pseudomonarchia Daemonum* (and forms its basis) and is essentially included wholesale in *The Book of Oberon*, but no extant copy pre-dating either of these two works can be found, despite being widely referenced. I've done my best, therefore, to be clear regarding my source information, and I enthusiastically encourage anyone interested in digging deeper into these grimoires to look to the bibliography provided in the end notes of this book.

One of the unique features of this Spirit index is the inclusion of new information about the Spirits derived from my own communications with members of the Lemegeton — most on my own, but some with a partner or my Coven. It's ironic, in a sense, that such a thing should be "new" and "unique," but the truth is that most treatments on this topic are a re-copying of the well-known Crowley/Mathers translation from the manuscripts in the British Museum. In the authentic grimoire tradition, though, each new author or transcriber was a Cunning person or Mage in their own right who had (and noted) their own experiences with the Spirits.

Each Spirit is depicted in a graphic form, as an aide for your visualization. Most of the depictions are digital collages made by me, but about 10 of them are artworks submitted by J. Blackthorn for the original printing. I am grateful for his talent, connection to the Spirits, and willingness to collaborate. I hope these visual depictions add something of value to your experience of the Legion.

BAEL - BY J. BLACKTHORN

Bael

Baal, Baall, Baell, Bail, Ball, Bel, Bell, Belli, Beltane Azazel, Beelzebub

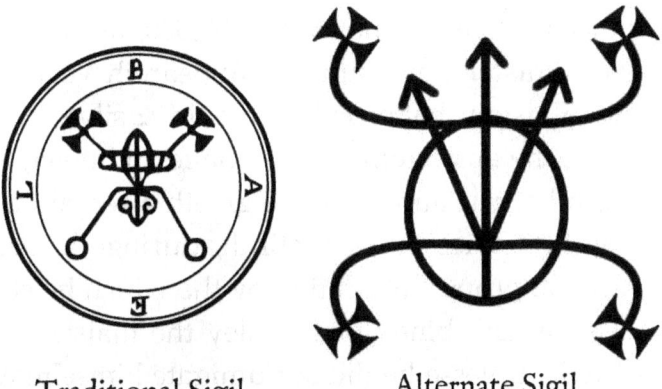

Traditional Sigil   Alternate Sigil

Number in Lemegeton	1
Rank in Lemegeton	King
Astrological Sign	
Planet	Mercury
Element	
Direction	East
Area(s) of Influence & Interest	Shapeshifting, Leadership, Empire-building, Cunning
Grimoires Which Mention	*Book of Incantations, The Discoverie of Witchcraft, The Magical Calendar, The*

Book of Spirits, The Book of the Office of Spirits, The Grand Grimoire, The Book of Oberon, Pseudomonarchia Daemonum, The Lesser Key of Solomon, Paradise Lost, and *Dictionnaire Infernal*

The Book of Oberon (Folger MS V.b.26, 1577) says ...

The second [devil] is called Bell, the which is Bellsabube, & he is the prince of devilles this Bell before the tyme of Solomon was thought to be the God Charon, whose Idoll was worshipped, & he was of the order of Cherubine, and 1,000,000, of divills or wicked spirrites doe minister unto him. He appeareth very beutifull, & giveth to the m[aiste]r that calleth him gold & silver & maketh expert in sciences, he appeareth well for halfe an hower, & giveth of e[a]ch demaund a true aunswere, he giveth a servant or ffamillier which shalbe in service verie duetifull, duringe a mans liff, but Nota he hath one proper Invocation by the which he shalbe called by: otherwise he hath bine wont to sley the maister Coniuror, & that in his Circle, unlesse he did suffumigate himselfe well, & that with amber, Lignum aloes, & masticke, & he most be called towards the east, where in he most be urged to doe his office & duetye.

Primus vocatur Baall & he hath power of love both of man & woman & to make a man invissible & he appeareth in the lyknes of a kinge, & he speaketh horsely.

Psuedomonarchia Daemonum (Johann Weyer, 1583) says ...

<Baell>. Their first <and principall> king (which is of the power of the east) is called *Baëll* who when he is conjured up, appeareth with three heads; the first, like a tode; the second, like a man; the third, like a cat. He speaketh with a hoarse voice, he maketh a man go invisible [and wise], he hath under his obedience and rule sixtie and six legions of divels.

The Grimorium Verum (1817) says ...

Conjuration for Beelzebuth. (Speak this 7 times)

"Beelzebuth, Lucifer, Madilon, Solymo, Saroy, Theu, Ameclo,

Sagrael, Praredun,

"Adricanorom, Martino, Timo, Cameron, Phorsy, Metosite, Prumosy, Dumaso, Elivisa,

"Alphrois, Fubentroty, Come, Beelzebuth, Amen."

The Lesser Key of Solomon, the Goetia (Thomas Rudd c. 1650; trans. & ed. Mathers/Crowley, 1904) says ...

The first Principal Spirit is a King ruling in the East, called Bael. He maketh thee to go Invisible. He ruleth over 66 Legions of Infernal Spirits. He appeareth in divers shapes, sometimes like a Cat, sometimes like a Toad, and sometimes like a Man, and sometimes all these forms at once. He speaketh hoarsely. This is his character which is used to be worn as a Lamen before him who calleth him forth, or else he will not do thee homage.

Dictionnaire Infernal (Jacques Collin de Plancy, 1863) says ...

Bael, demon cited in *Le Grand Grimoire*, as the head of all the infernal powers. It is also with him that Wierus begins the inventory of his famous *Pseudomononarchia demonum*. He calls Bael the first king of hell; his estates are the in the East. He is shown with three heads, of which one has the face of a toad, the other that of a man, the third that of a cat. His voice is raucous; but he is well formed. He repays those who invoke him with cunning and slyness and teaches them how to become invisible at need. Sixty six legions obey him. Is he the same as Baal?

Belzebuth or Belzebub or Belzebuth, Prince of demons, according to the scriptures; foremost in power and crime after Satan, according to Milton; chief of the infernal empire, according to most demonographers. His name signifies "Lord of the Flies." Bowden claims that he is no longer seen in his temple. He was the most revered god of the Canaanites, who sometimes represented him with the figure of a fly, more often with attributes of a sovereign power. He rendered oracles, and King Ochozias consulted him over a troubling malady; he was severely reprimanded for this by the prophet Elijah.

One attributed to him the power to deliver men from flies who ruined the harvest.

Almost all the demonomaniacs regard him as the sovereign of the gloomy empire; and each depicts him colored by his own imagination. Milton gives him an imposing aspect and high wisdom breathes on his face. One says he is as high as a tower; another of a size equal to our own; some give him the form and figure of a snake; in that form he is also seen with feminine traits.

The monarch of hell, said Pallingene, in *Zodiaco vitae*, is of a prodigious size, seated on an immense throne surrounded by a ring of fire. He has a swollen chest, bloated face, flashing eyes, raised eyebrows and a menacing air. He has extremely large nostrils and two great horns on his head. He is black like a Moor; two vast batlike wings are attached to his shoulders; he has two large duck feet, a lion's tail, and shaggy hair from his head to his feet.

Some say greater than Belzebuth is Priapus; others like Porphyri confuse him with Bacchus. Some believed that they found in him the Belbog or Belbach (white god) of the Slavs, because his bloody image was always covered with flies, like the Belzebuth of the Syrians. One said also that he was the same as Pluto. It is more reasonable to believe that he is Bael, whom Wierus made emperor of hell; all the more so since Belzebuth is not found by that name in his inventory of the infernal monarchy.

One sees in Solomon's *Clavicules* that Belzebuth appears sometimes in monstrous form, like that of an enormous calf or a goat with a long tail; nonetheless, he is often shown with the face of an ugly fly. He appeared to Faust "dressed like a bee and with two dreadful ears and his hair painted in all colors with a dragon's tail." The Marechel of Retz saw him as a leopard. When he was angry, one swears that he breathed fire and howled like a wolf. Finally, sometimes Asteroth appears at his side in the form of an ass.

Additional insight unlocked with the Witches' Key ...

S tells us, "Bael is a great magician and serves Azazel (the Witch Father) in all things. He knows much magic. The teachings of Azazel are his domain, which is why he is number 1 among the 72. He is said to make the Adept to go invisible. This is because he has mastery over shape-shifting and masking. Make-up is a form of masking."

Bael comes in many shapes and under many guises. Dog, cat, and toad are his most commonly seen animal forms, although he does reveal himself to some conjurers in the shape of a dragon. Any Witch who wishes to know him well should pay special attention to the symbolism and lore that is often attributed to these animals. He also appears as a man — a king. S says, "He is ugly but strong. He has horns upon his head. He speaks hoarsely."

He is a thundering, magick-wielding, monarch-maker. He is able to help ambitious and visionary Witches establish their own empires. He has grand scope and reach, and he is well suited to Witches who have big goals and are ready to pursue them. Be warned: he will blast obstacles out of your path including the obstacles and diversions you enjoy and use as a safety net.

He made two notable appearances in the English Witch trials. The first is in the case of the Device family in the village of Pendle. He appeared here as a black dog. They called him Ball (like the toy), perhaps not being aware of Baal. He is loyal to a family line, if the family holds true to the Craft. He had been the Familiar of Elizabeth Device, while Dantalion (whom they called Dandy and saw also as a black dog) had been in relationship with James Device. These are Spirits number 1 and 71 respectively in the Lemegeton, and it is not uncommon for them to work together in a group.

We also see Bael acting as a Familiar to Elizabeth Chandler of Huntingdonshire. In this case, he is seen as inspirited a log, and Chandler knew him under the name Beelzebub. Here again, he is working in cooperation with another Spirit, as Chandler keeps an inspirited twig called Trullibub.

Bael is old. He is Beltane-Azazel, Lord of the East and rising sun.

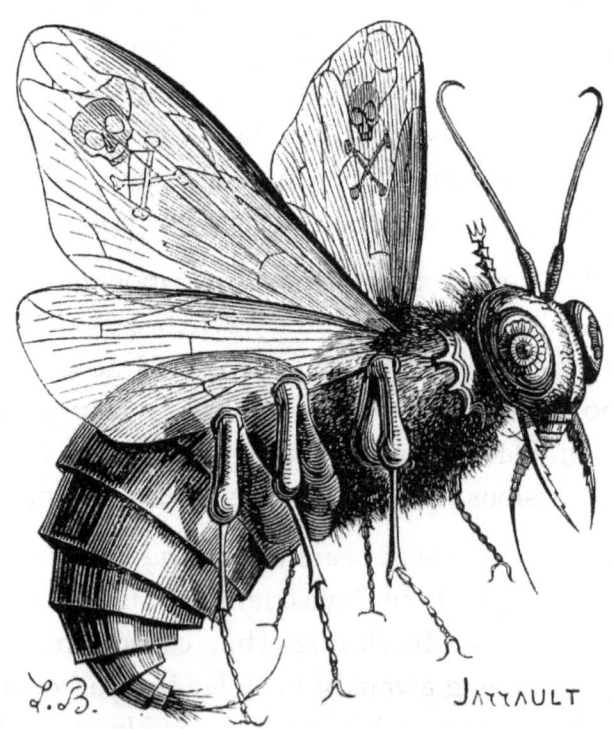

AGARES- BY LAURELEI BLACK

Agares

Acharos, Agaros, Agreas, Aguares, Aharas

Traditional Sigil   Alternate Sigil

Number in Lemegeton   2

Rank in Lemegeton   Duke

Astrological Sign

Planet   Mars

Element

Direction

Area(s) of Influence & Interest   Athletics, Languages, Earthquakes

Grimoires Which Mention   *Book of Incantations, The Discoverie of Witchcraft, Book of Treasure Spirits, The Book of Spirits, The Book of the Office of Spirits, The Grand Grimoire, The Book of Oberon, Pseudomonarchia Daemonum, The Lesser Key of Solomon,* and *Dictionnaire Infernal*

The Book of Oberon (Folger MS V.b.26, 1577) says ...

Acharos, vel [=or] Aharas, a duke & he is under the kinge of the east, he appeareth willingly like an old man, & his office is to teache all languages, & he causeth them that be rune awaye to come againe, & under him are 29 legions.

Agaros, he can teach all manner of languages, & tonges, he cane bringe, againe a fugitive or one rune awaye, & can promote to dignitye & worshipe, & appeareth in lykenes of an old man ridinge upon a cockeadrill.

Psuedomonarchia Daemonum (Johann Weyer, 1583) says ...

The first duke under the power of the east, <is named *Agares*,> he commeth up mildile [i.e. he appears willingly] in the likenes of a faire old man, riding upon a crocodile, and carrieng a hawke on his fist; hee teacheth presentlie all maner of toongs, he fetcheth backe all such as runne awaie, and maketh them runne that stand still; he overthroweth all dignities <supernaturall and temporall,> hee maketh earthquakes, [lit. "and makes spirits of the earth dance"] and is of the order of vertues, having under his regiment thirtie one legions.

The Lesser Key of Solomon, the Goetia (Thomas Rudd c. 1650; trans. & ed. Mathers/Crowley, 1904) says ...

The Second Spirit is a Duke called Agreas, or Agares. He is under the Power of the East, and cometh up in the form of an old fair Man, riding upon a Crocodile, carrying a Goshawk upon his fist, and yet mild in appearance. He maketh them to run that stand still, and bringeth back runaways. He teacheth all Languages or Tongues presently. He hath power also to destroy Dignities both Spiritual and Temporal, and causeth Earthquakes. He was of the Order of Virtues. He hath under his government 31 Legions of Spirits. And this is his Seal or Character which thou shalt wear as a Lamen before thee.

Dictionnaire Infernal (Jacques Collin de Plancy, 1863) says ...

Aguares, Grand Duke of the eastern part of hell. He is shown as a lord drawn by wires riding on the back of a crocodile, a sparrow hawk at his fist. He makes deserters return to the charge on the side that he protects and puts the enemy to flight. He dignifies them, teaches all languages, and makes dance the Earth spirits. This chief of the demons is of the Order of the Virtues; he has under his laws 31 legions.

Additional insight unlocked with the Witches' Key ...

He serves Ares. Agares is an athlete. Classic descriptions of Agares show him "riding upon a crocodile, carrying a goshawk upon his fist, and yet mild in appearance." S tells us, "the crocodile is a symbol for Typhon. He has the power to ground chaos. The bird is a symbol for sport." However, he doesn't actually appear before the Conjurer with these animals. "He just comes as a person. He's not ugly or old. He looks as a fighter would look in his prime."

He helps people develop their athletic abilities, and he is a master of all feats of physical prowess. He is reported to bring back runaways, but this was a reference to enslaved people who had escaped. If you need to bring home a runaway child, pet, or lover, there are better Spirits for that task.

He teaches all languages or tongues quickly. He helps you if you're trying to learn a new language. (There are spirits that help you speak in tongues, but Agares isn't one of them.)

"Very physical is Agares, hence his association with earthquakes."

He is very well suited to working with athletes, physical trainers, fitness coaches, and influencers who promote exercise programs. Because he is so focused on the physical being, it is too easy to say he is shallow or not relevant in a spiritual way. However, his commitment to health and fitness is of a spiritual nature, in his own way. "The vessel and the Spirit are bound," he says. "Partners wed."

VASSAGO - BY LAURELEI BLACK

Vassago

Vsagoo, Vzago

Traditional Sigil   Alternate Sigil

Number in Lemegeton	3
Rank in Lemegeton	Prince
Astrological Sign	
Planet	Moon
Element	Water
Direction	
Area(s) of Influence & Interest	Divination, Scrying, Visions; Invisibility; Hidden Things
Grimoires Which Mention	*Book of Incantations*, *Book of Treasure Spirits*, *The Book of the Office of Spirits*, *The Book of Oberon*, and *The Lesser Key of Solomon*

The Book of Oberon (Folger MS V.b.26, 1577) says ...

Vsagoo, magnus preses, he appeareth like an Aungell & is Just & true, in all his doeinges, he giveth the love of woemen, & telleth of hidd treasures, & hath under him 20 legions.

Vzago, whoe takinge humaine forme, hath power to make one wise & invissible, & to chaunge mann into another forme, or liknes, he getteth love & favour of all men, & giveth true aunswere of all thinges, he appeareth like an aungell, & is right true & faithfull, in all his doeinges

The Lesser Key of Solomon, the Goetia (Thomas Rudd c. 1650; trans. & ed. Mathers/Crowley, 1904) says ...

The Third Spirit is a Mighty Prince, being of the same nature as Agares. He is called Vassago. This Spirit is of a Good Nature, and his office is to declare things Past and to Come, and to discover all things Hid or Lost. And he governeth 26 Legions of Spirits, and this is his Seal.

Additional insight unlocked with the Witches' Key ...

This Spirit is of a good nature. He can see deep into time and is great at scrying. He works via visions. He rarely talks. He is for those who "see." However, he has many friends in the Legion, if the Conjurer wishes him to work in conjunction with other Spirits who do speak.

The moons in his seal show his vision power.

He looks like a man with big eyes and glasses. *S is doing a very unhelpful Professor Trelawney impression. Better psychic, but same big eyes and thick glasses. Eccentric seer look. Romani fortune teller putting on a show for the gorjas. Scarves, beads, big seeing Stone.*

Vassago is excellent with the past and future, but he isn't as skilled at uncovering messages or visions in the present. He isn't grounded at all, so "here and now" is a blind spot for him.

SAMIGINA - BY J. BLACKTHORN